AT HOME
IN
TWO LANDS

Intermediate Reading
and Word Study

William P. Pickett

Montclair State College
Passaic High School

NewburyHouse
A Division of HarperCollinsPublishers

To the Students from Many Lands
Whom I Have Taught and from
Whom I Have Learned Much

Director: Laurie E. Likoff
Full-Service Manager: Michael Weinstein
Production Coordinator: Cynthia Funkhouser
Production: Spectrum Publisher Services
Cover Design: Caliber Design Planning
Illustrations: Marsha Lacey
Compositor: Kachina Typesetting
Printer and Binder: Malloy Lithographing

NEWBURY HOUSE
A division of HarperCollins Publishers

Language Science
Language Teaching
Language Learning

At Home in Two Lands: Intermediate Reading and Word Study

Library of Congress Cataloging in Publication Data

Pickett, William P., 1931–
    At home in two lands : intermediate reading and word study /
  William P. Pickett.
        p.   cm.
    ISBN 0-06-632674-5
    1. English language—Textbooks for foreign speakers.   I. Title.
  PE1128.P468   1991
  428.2'4—dc20   91-7888
                                                          CIP

94 93 92 91 9 8 7 6 5 4 3 2 1

CONTENTS

VI. Seniors

PREFACE

Purpose

At **Home in Two Lands** is a reader and word-study text. It also serves as a springboard to discussion and is accompanied by a list of topics for written or oral presentations. **At Home in Two Lands** aims to:

1. Provide interesting reading material.
2. Expand a student's vocabulary.
3. Foster discussion and strengthen oral skills.
4. Link reading, discussion, and writing.
5. Increase a student's knowledge of prefixes, suffixes, homophones, and look-alikes.

Level

At Home in Two Lands is for intermediate students. Whether this means low intermediates or high intermediates depends on how these terms are defined and how students are grouped in a particular program.

Relationship to Far From Home

At Home in Two Lands is a sequel to **Far From Home** and is more advanced than the earlier text. **At Home** places more emphasis on discussion and a freer type of discussion than **Far From Home**. There are also pre-reading questions, longer stories, inference questions, and a list of topics for writing. These changes reflect modern trends, and a second edition of **Far From Home** will also incorporate them into its revised format.

Contents and Format

A. Lead Story

At Home is divided into six units with three lessons to a unit. The heart of each lesson is the lead story about a person or couple facing a problem or opportunity. The stories describe the successes and failures, the virtues and flaws of a wide range of people. Each story also has eight key words taught later in the lesson.

The stories are preceded by preview questions to activate the students' prior knowledge of the topic and to stimulate their curiosity. The stories are followed by comprehension questions. Some of these questions go beyond the text and require the reader to infer, judge, or speculate, as do the discussion questions later in the lesson.

B. Word Study

A mini-dictionary starts the word-study part of each lesson. The definition of each key word is followed immediately by a sentence or sentences using the word. A sentence-completion exercise complements the mini-dictionary. Each key word is used twice in the sentence-completion exercise.

After a second mini-dictionary and sentence-completion exercise, there is a modified cloze exercise with pre-reading questions. The cloze exercise tests and reinforces the eight key words of the lesson in a context that differs from that of the lead story.

C. Discussion

After the cloze exercise, there is a discussion section, "Sharing Information." The topics for discussion flow directly from the content of the lead and cloze story. The purpose of this section is to increase students' conversational skills and knowledge of the topics under discussion.

D. Topics for Writing

The discussion section is followed by suggested topics for compositions or oral presentations. This section is like a mini-appendix to the reading and discussion sections, enabling a class to go from reading, word study, and discussion to writing or oral presentations. This feature will be especially useful for multi-skill classes.

E. Word Families and Affixes

A word-family section follows. It lists the common words derived from the key words of the lesson and has the students use them in a sentence-completion exercise. After that, a concluding section of each lesson presents a suffix, or prefix, or homophones, or look-alikes, or shortened words.

F. Synonyms, Antonyms, and Review Tests

The final lesson of each unit also features a section on synonyms and antonyms. In addition, in the back of the book are provided tests that review and reinforce the twenty-four key words taught in each unit.

Word Selection

The key words taught in the stories were selected because of their frequency and importance, and because they were needed to tell the stories. Low-frequency words and idioms are explained in footnotes. Students need to know these key words to read widely, to understand TV and ordinary conversations, and to take college courses. They are not among the most common English words which students at this level already know, but their frequencies are high enough to make them extremely important.

A Special Blend

At Home in Two Lands differs from most word-study books and readers. It differs from the majority of word-study books because they generally do not emphasize high-interest readings. **At Home** features stories that make interesting reading apart from word study.

At Home differs from the majority of readers because of its focus on word study, a major need of almost all students. While many readers emphasize vocabulary expansion, they generally lack the concentration on word study found in **At Home in Two Lands.**

Answer Key and Audiocassette

An answer key is provided in the back of the book so students can check their answers. An audiocassette accompanies this book to facilitate its use in the classroom, in language labs, and at home.

Acknowledgments

I wish to thank my students at the Passaic Adult Learning Center, Passaic High School, Montclair State College, and the summer program of Harvard University for their help in field testing the material in this book.

I am also grateful to my colleagues, Denise Ceurvels and Debbie Laves, for their helpful suggestions. And I thank Susan Maguire, Laurie Likoff, and Cindy Funkhouser of Newbury House and Patti Brecht of Spectrum Publisher Services for their valuable assistance and encouragement. Finally I thank my wife Dorothy who reviewed all the stories and exercises of **At Home** and helped me improve them.

William P. Pickett

PRONUNCIATION KEY

To show the pronunciation of a word, most English dictionaries use symbols that are as close as possible to English spelling. The mini-dictionary section of **At Home in Two Lands** also uses these symbols. The symbols are listed below together with example words that have the sound the symbols represent.

The best way to learn to pronounce words is to listen to the pronunciation of native speakers and to imitate them. The mini-dictionary section of **At Home in Two Lands** provides pronunciation symbols because students do not always have the help of native speakers.

Vowel Sounds

a	**a**t, b**a**d	short a
ā	**ā**ge, l**ā**te	long a
â(r)	c**âr**e, b**âr**e	
ä	**ä**re, f**ä**ther	
e	**e**gg, b**e**d	short e
ē	**ē**ven, w**ē**	long e
i	**i**t, s**i**ck	short i
ī	**ī**ce, l**ī**fe	long i
o	**o**n, h**o**t	short o
ō	**ō**pen, g**ō**	long o
ô	**ô**ff, d**ô**g	
oo	b**oo**k, g**oo**d	
o͞o	t**o͞o**, f**o͞o**d	
u	**u**p, b**u**s	short u
ū*	**ū**se, m**ū**sic	long u
û(r)	t**ûr**n, h**ûr**t	
oi	v**oi**ce, n**oi**se	
ou	**ou**t, h**ou**se	

ə | **a**bout (ə-bout') / el**e**phant (el'ə-fənt) / pos**i**tive (poz'ə-tiv) / t**o**day (tə-dā') / ind**u**stry (in'dəs-trē)

ə is a special symbol that indicates a reduced a, e, i, o, or u. English frequently reduces vowel sounds that are not stressed. A reduced vowel sound is called a **schwa**.

*yo͞o is also a symbol for long u.

viii

Consonant Sounds

b	box, cab	p	pay, stop
ch	child, watch	r	run, dear
d	day, sad	s	sit, this
f	five, self	sh	shut, brush
g	give, bag	t	ten, but
h	hat	th	thin, teeth
j	job	*th*	*th*e, clo*th*e
k	kiss, week	v	vote, have
l	let, bill	w	want, grow
m	man, room	y	yes
n	not, sun	z	zone, buzz
ng	sing	zh	vision, garage

Unit One
Newlyweds

One

Falling in Love

Preview Questions

Discuss or think about these questions before reading the story.

1. How do most people meet their spouses?

2. What is romantic love? How does it differ from a general love of neighbor expressed in the sentence, "Love your neighbor as you love yourself"?

3. What are some signs that two people are in love? In other words, how do a couple know they're in love?

Falling in Love

Rita is twenty-four years old and she's married. Her parents are from Mexico, but she was born in Texas. She teaches computer science and math in a large public high school. It's not easy to work with teenagers, but Rita's a good teacher and the students like her. She's quite strict, but she's also fair and the students appreciate that. Rita could make more money in industry, but she loves teaching. It's very satisfying. After all, what's more important than helping young people learn?

Rita got married a year ago. She met her husband in a laundromat. She had taken her clothes out of the dryer and was **folding** them. She sensed that a man was **staring** at her. She looked up at him; he smiled and winked[1] at her. She looked the other way and **pretended** not to see him. She was a little angry, but she noticed he was good-looking and had a **charming** smile.

The man's name was Ken, and when she finished folding the clothes, he offered to help carry them to the car. At first she was **reluctant** to say yes, but he was nice and she had a lot of clothes, so she said okay. Ken introduced himself. That was the beginning of their friendship.

The next time Ken met Rita at the laundromat he offered to take her out to dinner. He took her to a nice restaurant and they had a wonderful time. They started spending a lot of time together. They played tennis, went dancing and bowling, and took long walks. They talked about their lives and their hopes for the future. Rita had never had such **tender** feelings for a man before. She thought about Ken all the time. She knew she was falling in love.

One night Ken and Rita went for a walk in the park. The moon was out and the stars were shining. It was a romantic evening. Ken and Rita sat on a bench at the edge of a small lake. "Do you mind if I ask you a question?" Ken asked. "Of course not," replied Rita. Ken was nervous, but he continued. "Will you marry me?" Rita's heart beat faster. She had thought he would never ask. "You know I will. I'm crazy about you."

Eight months later, Ken and Rita got married on a Saturday afternoon in June. The weather was perfect and Rita looked so pretty in her white dress and veil.[2] After they left the church, a limousine drove them to their reception. It wasn't a **fancy** reception, but their families and all of their friends were there, and they were **extremely** happy.

1. To **wink** is *to quickly shut and open one eye to show understanding or affection.*

2. A **veil** is *a covering for part of the head and face, made of net or other light material.*

affectionate adj.
love
tender, loving

3

I. Comprehension Questions

If the sentence is true, write T. If it's false, write F.

_____ 1. Rita is a good teacher and the students like her.

_____ 2. She is strict but fair with her students.

_____ 3. She fell in love with Ken immediately.

_____ 4. She noticed he was handsome.

_____ 5. She didn't hesitate to let him help with the clothes.

_____ 6. Rita and Ken had met before.

_____ 7. They like to play tennis, dance, and go bowling.

_____ 8. Rita spent a lot of time with Ken, but she wasn't sure she loved him.

_____ 9. She had been hoping he would propose.

_____ 10. It rained the day Ken and Rita got married.

II. MINI-DICTIONARY — PART ONE

1. **fold** (fōld) *verb:* to bend one part of something (usually paper or cloth) on top of the other
"Tony is **folding** the letter and putting it in an envelope."

2. **stare** (stâr) *verb:* to look at with fixed attention
"It's not polite to **stare** at people."

3. **pre·tend** (pri-tend´) *verb:* to act in a way that is different from the way you feel or are
"When Karen doesn't want to go to school, she **pretends** to be sick."

4. **charm·ing** (chärm´ing) *adjective:* very attractive; very pleasant
"Everyone likes Brenda. She's **charming**."

III.

Complete the sentences with these words. *If necessary, add an ending to the word so it forms a correct sentence,* for example, in sentence 3, **ed** must be added to **pretend** since the past tense is required. *Use each word twice.*

fold   stare   pretend   charming

1. I don't understand Charley. One minute he's _____*charming*_____ . The next minute he's unpleasant.
2. Will you help me to _____*fold*_____ these sheets?
3. Cliff _____*prentended*_____ to be angry, but he wasn't.
4. Everyone is _____*stared*_____ at the funny-looking hat Irene is wearing.
5. The children are _____*pretended*_____ to be monsters.
6. When we came back from the beach, we _____*folded*_____ the chairs and put them in the garage.
7. Pablo is fortunate. He has a _____*charming*_____ wife and a good job.
8. Why are you _____*stared*_____ at that man?

IV.   MINI-DICTIONARY — PART TWO

---

5. **re·luc·tant** (ri-luk′tənt) *adjective:* unwilling and slow to act
   "I'm **reluctant** to ask the boss for more money."

6. **ten·der** (ten′dər) *adjective:* warm and loving; soft; delicate
   "An infant needs lots of love and **tender** care."

7. **fan·cy** (fan′sē) *adjective:* special; high quality
   "Sue and Dick went to a **fancy** restaurant to celebrate their anniversary."

8. **ex·treme·ly** (ek-strēm′lē) *adverb:* very
   "The test was **extremely** difficult."

V.

Complete the sentences with these words. *If necessary, add an ending to the word so it forms a correct sentence. Use each word twice.*

reluctant   tender   fancy   extremely

1. When we were in Boston, we stayed in a ___fancy___ hotel. Of course, it was expensive.

2. The roast beef is ___tender___ . It tastes great.

3. The movie was ___extremely___ interesting.

4. We like to swim, but the water is so cold that we're ___reluctant___ to go in the pool.

5. It's ___extremely___ hot today.

6. I know I need the operation, but I'm ___reluctant___ to have it because I'm afraid.

7. Tim bought a ___fancy___ birthday cake for his daughter.

8. The little boy gave his mother a ___tender___ hug.

VI.   Preview Questions

Discuss or think about these questions before completing the story.

1. Do you rent an apartment or house? Or do you own a house?

2. Are you happy with the apartment or house that you live in? Is it big enough?

3. Part of the American dream is to own a house, but houses are very expensive. How much do you think the average house costs in the city or area where you live?

Complete the story with these words.

tender   folded   extremely   stared
charming   pretended   fancy   reluctant

Buying a House

Ivan and Ruth live in a small apartment in the middle of the city, but they have been saving money to buy a house. Since they don't have a lot of money, they're not looking for a _____fancy_____ house, but they want a yard, an extra bedroom, and more closet space. The closets in their apartment are _____extremely_____ small.

Yesterday a real-estate agent showed them a beautiful house in a quiet neighborhood. The house was _____charming_____ and so was the real-estate agent. Everything was going well until the agent gave them a paper describing the house and listing its price. Ivan _____stared_____ at the price. He couldn't believe his eyes. He _____folded_____ the paper and put it in his pocket. He knew they couldn't afford the house, but he was _____reluctant_____ to tell the real-estate agent until he discussed it with his wife. He _____pretended_____ that everything was okay.

When they got back to their apartment, Ruth said she loved everything about the house but its price. Ivan smiled, gave his wife a _____tender_____ kiss and said, "I'm sure that we can find a house just as nice that wouldn't cost so much."

VII.   Sharing Information

Discuss these questions in pairs or small groups.

A. Falling in Love

1. Rita is a good teacher. She is fair. What are some other qualities usually found in a good teacher?

2. Rita loves teaching. Do you think most teachers are satisfied with their profession? Explain your answer.

3. It's difficult to teach teenagers. Why?

4. Why is it difficult to be a teenager?

5. Everyone knows what love is, but it's not easy to put into words. Describe what love means to you by completing this sentence. Love is _____ _____ .

6. There are many different kinds of love, for example, romantic love ("Harry loves his girlfriend") and love of things ("I love my car"). Name some other kinds of love.

7. Rita was twenty-three and Ken was twenty-five when they married. What do you think is the *youngest* age at which a woman should marry? A man? What do you think is the *ideal* age for a woman to marry? A man?

B. Buying a House

8. What are the advantages of owning a house? Does the value of a house usually increase more quickly than money in the bank?

9. Most people buy a house by borrowing money from a bank. This loan is called a mortgage. What information does a bank ask for and check before giving a person a mortgage?

10. To buy a house, you must make a down payment; you must pay part of the cost of the house when you buy it. How much of a down payment do you think is necessary?

11. What does a real-estate agency do for a person who wishes to sell a house?

12. What qualities should a good real-estate agent have? Compare these qualities to those of a good teacher.

VIII. Topics for Writing or Discussion

Write a few lines, a paragraph, or a composition about one of these topics; or use them for further discussion or an oral report.

1. A Good Teacher
2. Teenagers
3. What Is Love?
4. How I Met My Spouse/Boyfriend/ Girlfriend
5. The Kind of Person I Want to Marry
6. My House
7. Buying a House
8. My Apartment
9. Renting an Apartment
10. My Neighborhood

IX. Word Families

Complete the sentences with the following words. If necessary, add an ending to the word so it forms a correct sentence. (adj. = adjective and adv. = adverb)

1. **to fold**   **folder** (noun)

   A. The secretary put the _____folder_____ in the filing cabinet.

   B. Gary _____folded_____ his wallet and put it in his pocket.

2. **to pretend**   **pretense** (noun)   **pretentious** (adj.)

   A. Nicole doesn't have much money, but she acts as if she were rich.
   She's very _____pretentious_____ .

   B. Karl _____pretents_____ to be tough, but he has a gentle heart.

   C. George doesn't like us and won't help. Don't let his kind words and
   _____pretense_____ fool you.

3. **charming** (adj.)   **charm** (noun)   **to charm**

   A. I like our new secretary; she's _____charming_____ and efficient.

   B. Ted _____charms_____ everyone he met at the party. He has a great
   personality.

   C. Amy is popular. She has a lot of _____charm_____ .

4. **reluctant** (adj.)   **reluctantly** (adv.)   **reluctance** (noun)

   A. I understand your _____reluctance_____ to go to the dentist, but you
   have to go.

B. Ralph ___reluctantly___ admitted he had thrown the baseball through the window.

C. Jane is ___reluctant___ to tell people her age, but I know she's fifty.

5. **tender** (adj.)   **tenderly** (adv.)   **tenderness** (noun)

A. Henry looked ___tenderly___ at his newborn son.

B. Jessica's skill and ___tenderness___ make her an excellent nurse.

C. Mm! This chicken is very ___tender___ .

6. **extremely** (adv.)   **extreme** (adj.)   **extreme** (noun)

A. It's difficult to exercise in ___extreme___ cold or heat.

B. I want to visit Japan, but it's ___extremely___ expensive.

C. One week Joan starves herself and the next week she eats constantly. She goes from one ___extreme___ to another.

X.   Building Words with im-

The negative prefix **in-** (see **Far From Home**, Chapter 16) is placed before adjectives and nouns and means **not** or **no**, for example, **incomplete, inexperience, insufficient**. Im- is used in place of **in-** before words beginning with **b, m,** or **p**. For example, **immature** means **not mature; imperfect** means **not perfect; imbalance** means **no balance.**

Adjective or Noun	Adjective or Noun
balance	imbalance
✓ mature	immature
measurable	immeasurable
mobile	immobile
moderate	immoderate
✓ moral	immoral
✓ mortal	immortal
movable	immovable
partial	impartial
patient	impatient
perfect	imperfect
personal	impersonal

10

Adjective or *Noun*	*Adjective* or *Noun*
polite	impolite
possible	impossible
practical	impractical
✓probable	improbable
proper	improper
pure	impure

Complete the sentences with these words.

impossible	impolite	imbalance	impure
immoral	impatient	immature	impartial

1. A judge should be ____impartial____ .
2. Roger is ____impolite____ . He never says please or thank you.
3. Stealing is ____immoral____ .
4. You'll get sick if you drink that water. It's ____impure____ .
5. I tried to get two tickets to the big game, but it was ____impossible____ .
6. Jim is twenty, but he often acts like a child. He's ____immature____ .
7. Paula doesn't like to wait for anything. She's ____impatient____ .
8. The United States imports more from Japan than it exports. This causes a large trade ____imbalance____ .

11

Two

Dividing the Housework

Preview Questions

Discuss or think about these questions before reading the story.

In many families, both husband and wife work. More and more married women are working. This raises some important questions.

1. Should a husband and wife divide the housework equally when both work?

2. Is that what usually happens, or does the wife usually do more than her share of the housework?

3. Do you think that men in the United States do more housework than men in most countries?

4. Are women usually neater than men? Are they usually more concerned with how their homes look?

Dividing the Housework

Both Ken and Rita have jobs so they divide the housework. She does some **tasks** and he does others. He does most of the cooking and she does most of the cleaning. She gives the house a **thorough** cleaning every Saturday. She vacuums the rugs, dusts the furniture, and sweeps the kitchen floor. She has a place for everything, and when she finishes cleaning, everything is in its place. Ken calls her "Miss Neat." He's also neat, much neater than most husbands, but sometimes he forgets to put things back where they belong.

Ken **seldom** cleans, but he cuts the grass, puts out the garbage, and shovels the snow in the winter. He's also extremely handy[1] and repairs things around the house. A year ago the hot water heater broke and he installed a new one himself. Last week the washer wouldn't work and he was able to fix it in a half-hour.

Ken usually cooks dinner. He learned to cook when he was young, and he likes to cook. Italian cooking is his specialty. He makes delicious lasagna and veal parmesan. Ken is a much better cook than Rita. She hates to cook. Most nights she watches TV while he cooks, and he watches TV while she does the dishes. He hates to do dishes.

Ken and Rita take pride in the way their house looks, but last night they had a **quarrel** about keeping the kitchen clean. When Ken came home from work, he was very tired. He had a tough day at work. Rita wasn't home yet. She had helped some students after school and then had gone food shopping.

Ken **tossed** his coat on the sofa and went to the kitchen for a snack. Ten minutes later the kitchen was a **mess**. There were **crumbs** on the floor, and dirty dishes and an empty soda bottle on the table. Ken went back to the living room and was reading the newspaper when Rita came home. As soon as he saw her, he remembered he hadn't cleaned up the kitchen and he knew she would be upset.

Ken was right. When Rita saw the kitchen, she hit the ceiling.[2] "Look at this mess," she said. "At least you could have put the dishes in the sink and the soda bottle in the garbage." "I **intended** to clean up," replied Ken. "But I was tired when I got home and just wanted to rest for a few minutes. I think you're making a mountain out of a molehill."[3] Their quarrel didn't last long. "Miss Neat" calmed down and Ken cleaned up the kitchen.

13

1. **Handy** means *good at fixing things*. Handy people are good with their hands.

2. **Hit the ceiling** is an idiom. It means *to become very angry*.

3. **To make a mountain out of a molehill** is an idiom. It means *to make a big problem out of a small one*. A mole is a small animal and the hill it makes is also small.

I.   Comprehension Questions

Answer these questions about the story. *Use your judgment to answer questions with an asterisk. Work in pairs or small groups.* The number in parentheses indicates the paragraph in which the answer is found.

  1. What special name does Ken have for Rita? (1)

*2. Do you think she likes this name? Explain your answer.

  3. Name four things Ken does in and around the house. (2)

*4. Do you think he does a fair share of the housework?

  5. What does Rita usually do when he cooks? (3)

  6. What did Ken and Rita quarrel about? (4)

  7. Why wasn't she home when Ken arrived? (4)

  8. What did he do when he came home from work? (5)

  9. What did he remember when he saw Rita? (5)

10. How did she react when she saw the kitchen? (6)

11. What excuse did Ken give her? (6)

*12. Do you think she was making a mountain out of a molehill?

II.   MINI-DICTIONARY — PART ONE

---

1. **task** (task) *noun:* work one must do; a job
   "Washing dishes is a **task** that few people like."

2. **sel·dom** (sel′dəm) *adverb:* rarely; not often
   "Jennifer is healthy. She **seldom** gets sick."

3. **thor·ough** (thûr′ō) *adjective:* complete
   "Our math test was **thorough**. It covered everything."

4. **quar·rel** (kwor′əl or kwôr′əl) *noun:* a fight with words; an
argument
verb: to fight with words; to argue
"Igor had a **quarrel** with his teenage son."

III.

Complete the sentences with these words. *If necessary, add an ending to the word so it forms a correct sentence. Use each word twice.*

thorough	task	quarrel	seldom

1. I ____seldom____ see my sister. She lives in California and I live in New York.

2. The accident report is ____thorough____. It describes in detail what happened.

3. I love my wife and she loves me, but we ____quarrel____ a lot.

4. A teacher's ____task____ is to help students to learn.

5. The doctor gave me a ____thorough____ examination.

6. We ____seldom____ go to the movies. We watch them on our VCR instead.

7. Raising children isn't an easy ____task____ .

8. Mark had a ____quarrel____ with his boss, and he almost lost his job.

IV.   *MINI-DICTIONARY — PART TWO*

---

5. **toss** (tôs) *verb:* to throw
noun: the act of throwing
"The fish was so small that Dan **tossed** it back into the lake."

6. **mess** (mes) *noun:* without order; not neat
"When are you going to clean your room? It's a **mess**."

7. **crumb** (krum) *noun:* very small pieces of bread, cake, etc.
"The children were eating cookies in the living room, and they left **crumbs** on the rug."

8. **in·tend** (in-tend´) *verb:* to plan; to want to
   "Randy and I **intend** to go to Europe this summer."

___

V.

Complete the sentences with these words. *If necessary, add an ending to the word so it forms a correct sentence. Use each word twice.*

toss **intend** **mess** **crumb**

1. We _____ intended _____ to play soccer, but it rained so hard we stayed home.

2. Linda usually puts bread _____ crumbs _____ on the chicken before baking it.

3. The room is still cold. _____ Toss _____ another piece of wood on the fire.

4. They had a rock concert in the park last night and left a

   _____ mess _____ .

5. _____ Toss _____ the ball to me!

6. My friends liked the cake. They ate every _____ crumb _____ .

7. John and Rose _____ intend _____ to sell their house and move to San Diego.

8. Everything we don't need is put in the basement. It's a _____ mess _____ .

VI. *Preview Questions*

Discuss or think about these questions before completing the story.

1. Do people with professional training often have to take low-paying jobs when they first go to live in another country? Why?

2. In the United States, where can a person who doesn't speak or understand English work?

3. Why is English a difficult language to learn?

4. Why is English difficult to pronounce and spell?

Complete the story with these words.

quarrel	crumbs	intends	seldom
mess	thorough	tosses	task

Another Quarrel

Roberto came to the United States two months ago. He's from Lima, Peru. He was an accountant there, but he knows very little English. He ___intends___ to go to school to learn English, but learning English is a difficult ___task___, and he doesn't have time now.

Roberto works in a restaurant cleaning tables. When the customers finish eating, the tables are a ___mess___. Roberto takes the dirty dishes to the kitchen, ___tosses___ the leftover food into the garbage, and goes back and brushes the ___crumbs___ off the table. He does a ___thorough___ job. The tables have to look nice before the next customers are seated.

Roberto ___seldom___ gets angry, but last night he had a ___quarrel___ with the manager of the restaurant about his salary. Roberto thinks he deserves more money, but the manager won't give him a raise. So he's looking for another job.

VII. Sharing Information

Discuss these questions in pairs or small groups.

A. Dividing the Housework

1. Can you cook? Who cooks where you live? How often do you cook? Are you a good cook?

2. The cooks or chefs in many restaurants are men, but most of the cooking at home is done by women. Why?

3. Who does the dishes where you live? Do you think doing the dishes is boring? Do you hate to do dishes?

4. Many men don't do their share of the housework. What's the reason? (A) They're lazy. (B) They think it's a woman's job. (C) They were spoiled by parents who didn't make them do any housework. (D) All of the above. Can you think of any other reason?

5. How neat are you? (A) Extremely neat? (B) Very neat? (C) Quite neat? (D) Not so neat? Is it possible to be too neat? Explain your answer.

6. Ken and Rita quarreled about keeping the kitchen clean. What are some other things married couples quarrel about?

7. Almost all couples quarrel at times. Why?

B. Another Quarrel

8. What country are you from? What is your first language?

9. Why is it difficult for adults to learn a second language? Why is it a lot easier for children to do so?

10. Roberto was an accountant. What does an accountant do? Does an accountant need a college education?

11. Do you think it will be easy for Roberto to find a job that pays more? Explain your answer.

12. How often do you get angry? (A) Seldom? (B) Sometimes? (C) Frequently?

13. At whom do you get angry?

14. Tell us something that other people do that makes you angry.

VIII. Topics for Writing or Discussion

Write a few lines, a paragraph, or a composition about one of these topics; or use them for further discussion or an oral report.

1. The Changing Roles of Men and Women in Modern Society
2. Miss Neat/Mr. Neat
3. A Quarrel
4. How My Husband/Wife Annoys Me
5. How My Friend/Roommate Annoys Me
6. English Is a Difficult Language
7. My First Job
8. My Favorite Restaurant
9. The Time I Got So Angry
10. What Makes Me Angry

IX. Word Families

Complete the sentences with the following words. If necessary, add an ending to the word so it forms a correct sentence. (adj. = adjective and adv. = adverb)

1. **thorough** (adj.)   **thoroughly** (adv.)   **thoroughness** (noun)

   A. Make sure you cook the pork ____thoroughly____ .

   B. Kirk is a good auto mechanic. He's known for his ____thoroughness____ .

   C. We learn a lot in Mrs. King's class. She's a ____thorough____ teacher.

2. **mess** (noun)   **messy** (adj.)   **messiness** (noun)

   A. I couldn't help but notice the ____messiness____ of my friend's apartment.

   B. My husband promised to clean up the yard, but it's still a ____mess____ .

   C. The children didn't pick up their toys. Their room is ____messy____ .

3. **crumb** (noun)   **to crumble**   **crummy*** (adj.)

   A. After the party, I vacuumed the rug. There were a lot of ____crumbs____ on it.

19

B. The movie was _____crummy_____ . We left in the middle of it.

C. The wall _____crumbled_____ when the truck hit it.

*Crummy means *not good; of poor quality*. Crummy is slang and should be used only informally.

4. **to intend**   **intent*** (noun)   **intention** (noun)   **intentional** (adj.)
   intentionally (adv.)   **unintentional** (adj.)   **unintentionally** (adv.)

A. Jeff didn't want the fire alarm to ring. He set it off ___unintentionally___ .

B. We _____Intend_____ to buy a new car soon.

C. My son broke a window, but it wasn't _____intentional_____ . It was an accident.

D. The _____intent_____ of most traffic laws is to prevent accidents.

E. I didn't mean to wake you up. It was _____unintentional_____ .

F. Ruth wanted to insult us. She did it _____intentionally_____ .

G. Ernie's advice didn't help us, but his _____intention_____ were good.

*Intent and intention are synonyms. Intent is preferred in legal contexts and is the best answer to sentence D.

X.   Building Words with il- and ir-

Instead of **in**, the negative prefixes **il-** and **ir-** are used before words beginning with **l** and **r**. For example, **illegal** means **not legal**; **illiterate** means **not literate**; **irregular** means **not regular**; **irresponsible** means **not responsible**.

Adjective	Adjective
legal	illegal
✓ legible	illegible
✓ legitimate	illegitimate
literate	illiterate
logical	illogical
✓ rational	irrational
regular	irregular
✓ relevant	irrelevant
religious	irreligious

20

Adjective	*Adjective*
replaceable	irreplaceable
resistible	irresistible
responsible	irresponsible
✓reverent	irreverent
✓reversible	irreversible

Complete the sentence with these words.

irreplaceable	✓illiterate	irrelevant	illegible
✓irregular	irreversible	✓illegal	✓irresponsible

1. We can't rely on Kevin. He's ___irresponsible___.
2. Betty can't read or write. She's ___illiterate___.
3. The past tense of **go** is **went**; it's an ___irregular___ verb.
4. Your comments have nothing to do with the topic we're discussing.
   They're ___irrelevant___.
5. It's ___illegal___ to fish without a license.
6. The fire at the museum destroyed many works of art. Most of them
   are ___irreplaceable___.
7. It hasn't rained in ten weeks. The damage to the crops is
   ___irreversible___.
8. Your handwriting is ___illegible___. I can't read it.

21

Three

A Thriving Business

Preview Questions

Discuss or think about these questions before reading the story.

1. What does a person need to start a business?

2. What are some of the advantages of having your own business? What are some disadvantages?

3. Do you think you would make a good businessman or businesswoman? Why or why not?

4. Would you like to have a business someday? If so, what kind of business?

A Thriving Business

Ken owns a bakery in a small shopping center and his business is **thriving**. The bakery is always crowded on the weekends. It has delicious cakes, cookies, and bread, and everything is fresh. Ken throws out or gives away anything that is **stale**. He knows how important it is to keep his customers happy, and he doesn't want anything in his bakery to be stale.

Shortly after Ken and Rita were married, she started to help out in the bakery on Sunday morning when it's the busiest. Now she also keeps the books, pays the bills, and makes out the deposit slips for the bank. She's very good at math and likes this type of work. Rita is a good businesswoman as well as a good teacher, and Ken is happy to have her share the responsibility of running the bakery.

The bakery is beginning to make a lot of money, but the work is hard and the hours are long. Sunday afternoon is the only time the bakery is closed. As soon as it closes, Ken and Rita go home and relax. They try not to talk about the bakery for the rest of the day. If the weather is nice, they take a walk or play tennis. If it's bad or very cold, they rent a movie and watch it on their VCR.

They always eat out on Sunday night. They're too tired to cook or do the dishes. Ken likes to go to Italian restaurants and compare their cooking with his own. Rita prefers Spanish food. She especially likes paella* and all types of fish. Ken and Rita dream of opening a restaurant someday, but they're practical and know they have to concentrate on the bakery for now.

The bakery has had a **steady** increase in business ever since it opened five years ago. There's only one problem with it; it's too small, and people have to wait too long. **Despite** the long wait, the customers keep coming back. They know it's the best bakery in the city. Last week Ken **hired** another baker and cashier.

Ken is also planning to **expand** his store. He's going to talk to an architect this afternoon. They'll go over Ken's plans and discuss how much the project will cost. With the help of the architect and Rita, he's going to prepare a **budget**. Then he plans to go to the bank and apply for a loan. After he gets it, he'll hire a contractor. Expanding the store is a big **challenge**. It won't be easy, but Ken and Rita know they can do it.

*__Paella__ is a popular Spanish dish. It is a combination of rice, fish, meat, and vegetables.

I. Comprehension Questions

If the sentence is true, write T. If it's false, write F.

__T__ 1. Ken's business is doing very well.

__F__ 2. Sometimes the cake and bread in his bakery are stale.

__F__ 3. Ken keeps the books and pays the bills.

__T__ 4. Rita is a good businesswoman.

__F__ 5. The bakery is closed on Mondays.

__F__ 6. Ken and Rita eat out on Sunday so they can relax and talk about the bakery.

__T__ 7. Rita likes Spanish food and fish.

__T__ 8. Ken's bakery is the best in the city.

__T__ 9. Rita and the architect are going to help Ken prepare a budget.

__F__ 10. Expanding the store will be easy.

II. MINI-DICTIONARY — PART ONE

---

1. **thrive** (thrīv) *verb:* to do very well
   "Francisco is very happy. His restaurant is **thriving**."

2. **stale** (stāl) *adjective:* not fresh anymore; not new
   "This bread is a week old. It's **stale**."

3. **stead·y** (sted′ē) *adjective:* continuous; not changing or stopping
   "It's been very dry lately. We need a **steady** rain."

4. **de·spite** (di-spīt′) *preposition:* in contrast or opposition to
   "Sophie is eighty-nine today. She's in good health **despite** her age."

III.

Complete the sentences with these words. *If necessary, add an ending to the word so it forms a correct sentence. Use each word twice.*

stale   despite   thrive   steady

24

1. ___Despite___ many problems, Melissa is always cheerful.

2. Steve is learning how to play the piano, and he's making

    ___steady___ progress.

3. Orange trees ___thrive___ in hot weather.

4. This beer tastes terrible. It's ___stale___.

5. The newer sections of the city are ___thriving___, and the older ones are struggling.

6. Leo is only five feet six. ___Despite___ his size, he's the best basketball player on the team.

7. Teachers don't get paid a lot, but they have a ___steady___ income.

8. Of course we know that Pete and Donna are moving. That's

    ___stale___ news.

IV. MINI-DICTIONARY — PART TWO

5. **hire** (hīr) *verb:* to give someone a job; to employ someone
     "The ice-cream store **hires** extra help during the summer."

6. **ex·pand** (ik-spand' or ek-spand') *verb:* to make or become bigger
     "The city **expanded** the park so the children would have more room to play."

7. **bud·get** (buj'it) *noun:* a plan for spending money
                  verb: to make a plan for spending money
     "Salaries are the biggest item in most **budgets**."

8. **chal·lenge** (chal'ənj) *noun:* something that is difficult to do; something that requires great effort
                  verb: to invite someone to compete in a game, etc.: to question a statement or action
     "Climbing the mountain was a **challenge**."
     "I **challenge** you to a game of tennis."

V.

Complete the sentences with these words. *If necessary, add an ending to the word so it forms a correct sentence. Use each word twice.*

budget   hire   challenge   expand

1. Sandra is ambitious. She likes a _____ challenge _____ .
2. I'm going to _____ hire _____ someone to paint the house. I can't do it myself.
3. We didn't _____ budget _____ enough money for travel, so we can't go to California this year.
4. When water freezes, it _____ expands _____ .
5. My new job is a _____ challenge _____ , but I can handle it.
6. The company _____ hired _____ another bookkeeper last week.
7. Some families have a _____ budget _____ , but most don't bother.
8. Our library doesn't have enough space. We're going to _____ expand _____ it.

VI.   Preview Questions

Discuss or think about these questions before completing the story.

1. Are salaries in the construction industry high? How steady is the work?

2. Do you think Florida would be a good place for a construction worker to look for a job? Explain your answer.

3. Why do so many people move to Florida?

Complete the story with these words.

stale   ✓ expanding   ✓ steady   budget
✓ hire   ✓ despite   challenge   ✓ thriving

Looking for Work in the Construction Business

Tony is a construction worker and he's just arrived in Miami, Florida. He came

to Florida because he couldn't find a _____ steady _____ job where he lived.

_____Despite_____ the high pay in the construction industry, Tony hasn't been doing well. He's been unemployed for several months.

The population of Florida is _____expanding_____ rapidly, and its economy is _____thriving_____ , so there are lots of construction jobs there. People need more houses and condominiums. Tony has a job interview tomorrow, and he's pretty sure the company will _____hire_____ him.

The company plans to build three hundred condominiums in a year. Building them in such a short time is a _____challenge_____ , but the president of the company is confident they can do it if they find enough good workers.

Right now Tony is eating supper at a cheap diner and thinking about his interview. The food is terrible. The rolls are _____stale_____ , the potatoes are cold, and the steak is tough. He would have eaten at a good restaurant, but he doesn't have much money and he's living on a tight _____budget_____ . If he get's the job, he's going to celebrate by eating in one of Miami's better restaurants.

VII. *Sharing Information*

Discuss these questions in pairs or small groups.

A. A Thriving Business

1. How often do you go to a bakery? What do you buy? Do you have a favorite bakery? If so, what's its name?

2. Thirty years ago people baked at home more than they do today. Why? Do you ever bake at home? What do you bake?

3. Ken and Rita work long hours at the bakery and make a lot of money. Do most people who have their own business work long hours? How many make a lot of money? Most? Many? Some? A few?

4. Rita's work at the bakery is a second job. Why do teachers often have second jobs?

5. All governments and big businesses have budgets. Is it also a good idea for individuals and families to have one? Why? Do you think very many do? If they don't, why not?

B. Looking for Work in the Construction Business

6. If you're working, what is your job? Do you like it? How did you get your job?

7. Did you ever have a job interview? What was it like?

8. What questions do interviewers usually ask? What questions do those interviewed usually ask?

9. Can friends and relatives sometimes help a person get a job? How?

10. How can newspapers help?

11. How do employment agencies help? Who pays them?

12. What is a resumé? What kinds of jobs require one?

13. What can people do to increase their opportunities for a good job? What type of training or education would help you?

VIII. *Topics for Writing or Speaking*

Write a few lines, a paragraph, or a composition about one of these topics; or use them for further discussion or an oral report.

1. My Business
2. Advantages and Disadvantages of Owning a Business
3. How I Plan to Become Rich
4. Getting a Loan
5. A Budget
6. How to Look for a Job
7. How I Got My Job
8. A Job Interview
9. The Job I Want and What I Must Do to Get It
10. A Resumé

IX. Word Families

Complete the sentences with the following words. If necessary, add an ending to the word so it forms a correct sentence. (adj. = adjective and adv. = adverb)

1. **steady** (adj.)   **steadily** (adv.)   **steadiness** (noun)

   A. It snowed ____steadily____ for twenty-four hours.

   B. Ron wasn't a great baseball player, but his ____steadiness____ helped his team a lot.

   C. A ____steady____ stream of people were leaving the train station.

2. **despite** (preposition)   **in spite of*** (preposition)

   Delia works very hard **despite** her poor health.

   Delia works very hard **in spite of** her poor health.

   ***In spite of** has the same meaning as **despite** and is used in the same way. Both are prepositions.

3. **to expand**   **expanse** (noun)   **expansion** (noun)   **expansive** (adj.)

   A. It's easy to get to know Marlene. She has an ____expansive____ personality.

   B. Lee is taking a course in the history of the United States. He wants to ____expand____ his knowledge of the country.

   C. When the state built the highway, they bought enough property to allow for ____expansion____ .

   D. The first time we saw the farm we were amazed by its ____expanse____ . It was huge.

4. **challenge** (noun or verb)   **challenger** (noun)   **challenging** (adj.)

   A. Mike Tyson was the champion; his opponent was the ____challenger____ .

   B. Joyce ____challenged____ her friend to a race and won.

   C. The work of a lawyer is ____challenging____ .

X.

A. Synonyms

Next to each sentence, write a **synonym** *for the underlined word or phrase. If necessary, add an ending to the synonym.*

✓ thrive	✓ extremely	✓ task	✓ thorough
✓ quarrel	✓ intend	✓ toss	pretend

1. Neil isn't hurt. He's <u>acting</u>. _____pretended_____
2. We loved the show. It was <u>very</u> funny. _____extremely_____
3. My brother and I had a <u>fight</u> last night. _____quarrel_____
4. This grammar gives a <u>complete</u> explanation of English tenses.
   _____thorough_____
5. Our club is <u>doing very well</u>. _____thriving_____
6. Janet <u>plans</u> to paint her bedroom. _____intend_____
7. Jerry <u>threw</u> the empty can into the garbage. _____toss_____
8. A doctor's <u>job</u> is to care for sick people. _____task_____

B. Antonyms

Using the words below, complete each sentence with an **antonym** *of the underlined word. If necessary, add an ending to the antonym.*

stale	✓ hire	expand	✓ steady
✓ seldom	despite	✓ fancy	reluctant

1. Gabe stops at the bar for an <u>occasional</u> drink, but his cousin is a
   _____steady_____ customer.
2. Some factories are <u>firing</u> workers, but we're _____hiring_____ them.
3. Sylvia likes to wear <u>plain</u> dresses, not _____fancy_____ ones.
4. Ben <u>frequently</u> plays golf. Steve _____seldom_____ does.
5. Edith is <u>eager</u> to move, but her husband is _____reluctant_____ .

6. These donuts are ___*stale*___ . Can you get us some <u>fresh</u> ones?

7. ___*Despite*___ poor work at the beginning of the semester, I passed <u>because of</u> a high grade on the final exam.

8. When air is cooled, it <u>contracts;</u> when it's heated, it ___*expands*___ .

XI. Building Words with -ive (-ative)

The suffix **-ive (-ative)** is added to verbs and nouns and forms an adjective or noun. **-Ive (-ative)** usually means **inclined to**, for example, **active** means **inclined to act; talkative** means **inclined to talk; cooperative** means **inclined to cooperate. -Ive (-ative)** can also mean **one who**, for example, **a detective** is **one who detects** and a **representative** is **one who represents.**

Verb or *Noun*	*Adjective* or *Noun*
act	active
communicate	communicative
cooperate	cooperative
create	creative
decide	decisive
defect	defective
detect	detective
expand	expansive
expense	expensive
imagine	imaginative
inform	informative
invent	inventive
protect	protective
represent	representative
talk	talkative

contract ⟷ expand

Complete the sentences with these words.

✓ decisive   ✓ active   ✓ cooperative   talkative
✓ protective   defective   ✓ representative   ✓ expensive

1. Beth is ____cooperative____ . She'll help us.

2. I want to buy a Mercedes, but they're too ____expensive____ .

3. Lenny is ____active____ . He never keeps quiet.

4. This pen is new, but it won't write. It's ____defective____ .

5. Jill is ____decisive____ . She makes up her mind quickly.

6. I can't go to the meeting, but I'm sending a ____representative____ .

7. Brendan is very ____talkative____ . He's always doing something.

8. Jackie won't let her son go to the park with the other children. She's too ____protective____ .

Unit Two
Teenagers

Four

A Great Basketball Player

Preview Questions

Discuss or think about these questions before reading the story.

1. What sports do you like? Which is your favorite?

2. What sports have you played? Do you play any now?

3. What sports do you watch on TV?

4. What are the most popular sports in the United States? In another country you know?

A Great Basketball Player

Ray is seventeen years old and is in his last year of high school. He loves sports and is an **outstanding** athlete. He plays baseball in the spring and summer. He's a good hitter, is fast, and has a strong arm. Last season he hit ten home runs. However, basketball is his favorite sport.

Ray is only five feet, nine inches tall, but he's a great basketball player. He can pass and shoot well, and he generally scores more than twenty points a game. Last year he scored forty points in the game in which his high-school team won the state championship. He's easily the best player on his team, and one of the best in the state.

Several colleges have already offered Ray a basketball scholarship so it won't cost him a penny to go to college except for personal expenses. Ray is very happy about this. His family doesn't have much money and it's expensive to go to college. He wants to study to be an engineer as well as to play basketball. Some athletes aren't good students, but Ray is. He likes to read and study, and he did very well on his College Board Examinations.[1] He will probably go to Duke University because they have one of the best basketball programs in the country, and they expect their players to study hard.

Friday afternoon Ray and some of his friends were playing basketball in the gym. It was almost six o'clock and everyone was getting tired. Suddenly Ray **twisted** his ankle and had to stop playing. He **limped** off the court; he was in a lot of pain. His friends were afraid he might have broken his ankle and wanted to take him to a doctor, but Ray is **stubborn**. He **refused** to go. "I will be all right in a day or two," he said. One of his friends had a car and drove him home.

When Ray got home, he **soaked** his ankle in hot water and Epsom salts.[2] This helped a lot, but the ankle still hurts. Ray can walk but he limps a little, and he won't be able to play basketball for two weeks. He's **disappointed**. He thought his ankle would **heal** more quickly. The high-school team starts practice tomorrow, and he will miss the first two weeks of practice. However, the first game of the season is still a month away. The coach wants him to rest now so that he'll be ready for the first game.

1. Many colleges require applicants to take a special entrance exam called the College Board Examination.

2. **Epsom salts** is a white mineral powder that is mixed with hot water and used to reduce swellings.

I. Comprehension Questions

Answer these questions about the story. *Use your judgment to answer questions with an asterisk. Work in pairs or small groups.* The number in parentheses indicates the paragraph in which the answer is found.

1. Why is Ray a good baseball player? (1)

2. What's his favorite sport? (1)

*3. Why is being tall an advantage in basketball?

4. What two basketball skills does Ray have? (2)

*5. What are some personal expenses a college student would have?

6. What does Ray want to do in college? (3)

*7. How much, do you think, it costs a year to attend and live at a good private college? At a state college or university?

*8. Do you think Ray should have gone to see a doctor? Explain your answer.

9. Why couldn't his friends get him to go to a doctor? (4)

10. What did Ray do when he got home? (5)

11. Why is he disappointed? (5)

12. How many weeks will he be able to practice before the first game? (5)

II. MINI-DICTIONARY — PART ONE

1. **out·stand·ing** (out·stan′ding) *adjective:* very good; excellent; better than others
   "It's a great restaurant. The food and the service are **outstanding**."

2. **twist** (twist) *verb:* to turn: to injure by turning
   noun: the act of twisting
   "Drive slowly. This road is narrow and it **twists** a lot."
   "Give the cap a **twist**. It'll come off."

3. **limp** (limp) *verb:* to walk with a step that is not even
   "Laura was in an accident a week ago. She hurt her foot and she's still **limping**."

4. **stub·born** (stub′ərn) *adjective:* having a strong will; unwilling to change

"Andy is very **stubborn**. He'll never change his mind."

III.

Complete the sentences with these words. *If necessary, add an ending to the word so it forms a correct sentence. Use each word twice.*

stubborn   **twist**   **limp**   **outstanding**

1. Dianne always gets a hundred on her tests. She's an _____ student.

2. _____ the bulb a little tighter.

3. Why are you _____ ? What happened to your leg?

4. Marty won't listen to anyone. He's as _____ as a mule.

5. I didn't sleep well last night. I _____ and turned most of the night.

6. *Chorus Line* was an _____ musical.

7. It's hard to get Sara to accept any new ideas. She's _____ .

8. When the coach saw that Abdul was _____ , he took him out of the game.

IV.   MINI-DICTIONARY — PART TWO

---

1. **re·fuse** (ri·fyo͞oz′) *verb:* to be unwilling to do or accept something
   "Glen **refused** to help us."

2. **soak** (sōk) *verb:* to place something in water and leave it there for a period of time
   "I'm going to **soak** these clothes before I wash them. They're very dirty."

3. **dis·ap·point** (dis`ə·point′) *verb:* to fail to satisfy the hopes or wishes of
   "The team didn't play well. They **disappointed** their fans."

4. **heal** (hēl) *verb:* to return to a healthy condition; to get better
   "Debbie broke her arm, but it's **healing** nicely."

V.

Complete the sentences with these words. *If necessary, add an ending to the word so it forms a correct sentence. Use each word twice.*

soak   heal   disappoint   refuse

1. I try to do well in school. I don't want to _____ my parents.

2. It started to rain hard and Pat didn't have an umbrella. She got

   _____ .

3. My friend wanted me to lie, but I _____ .

4. Shawn hurt his shoulder a month ago, and it hasn't _____ yet.

5. The workers were _____ by the small pay increase.

6. Ann got angry when her son _____ to pick up his toys.

7. If you put this cream on your sunburn, it'll _____ quickly.

8. I hurt my thumb. I'm going to _____ it in warm water.

VI.   Preview Questions

Discuss or think about these questions before completing the story.

1. Wrestling is an interesting sport for a number of people. Do you find it interesting?

2. Some people like to watch wrestling on TV. Do you? Do you watch it much?

3. Did you ever go to a wrestling match? If so, where?

Complete the story with these words.

soaked	outstanding	twisted	stubborn
limping	refused	healed	disappointed

Wrestling

Wrestling is one of Paul's favorite sports, and he's an average wrestler. The other

day he was wrestling with his friend Sam. Sam is an _____

wrestler and he was winning the match, but Paul _____ to quit.

He's very _____ .

Sam _____ Paul's arm and threw him down on the mat. Paul was able to get up and keep wrestling, but the contest wasn't close. Paul was _____ that he couldn't do better.

When Paul got up the next morning, his muscles were sore. He couldn't walk without _____ . So he sat in the bathtub for forty-five minutes and _____ his sore muscles.

He also had a cut over his eye. Fortunately, the cut wasn't deep and it _____ in a few days.

VII. *Sharing Information*

Discuss these questions in pairs or small groups.

A. A Great Basketball Player

1. What is the value of sports?
2. Do high schools and colleges in other countries place as much emphasis on sports as those in the United States?
3. Do you think there's too much emphasis on high-school and college sports in the United States?
4. What is an athletic scholarship? Why do many colleges in the United States give them? What are some arguments in favor of them? What are some arguments against them?
5. Are you reluctant to go to a doctor even when you know you should? If so, why?
6. Ray likes to read and study. Do you like to read? Do you read much? What kinds of books do you like to read?
7. What magazine(s) and newspaper(s) do you read?

8. Do you like to study?

9. How stubborn are you? Not at all? A little stubborn? Quite stubborn? Very stubborn? Do you think it's good to be a little stubborn? Explain.

B. Wrestling

10. Professional wrestling in the United States is part sport and part acting; for example, wrestlers sometimes pretend they've been hurt when they haven't. Some people don't like professional wrestling because of the pretending. How do you feel about this?

11. Do you admire Paul for his courage, for trying hard, or do you think he was foolish to wrestle with someone so good?

12. Do you think we place too much emphasis on winning in sports? What do you think of these statements? "When we play a game, winning is the most important thing." "Winning is not important, it's how you play the game."

13. Exercise is important for everyone. Why is it so important? Do you think people spend too much time watching sports, especially on TV, and too little time playing them?

14. How much exercise do you get? A lot? Some? Very little? Do you swim, jog, hike, skate, or bike? Do you get any other type of exercise?

VIII. *Topics for Writing or Discussion*

Write a few lines, a paragraph, or a composition about one of these topics; or use them for further discussion or an oral report.

1. The Value of Sports
2. My Favorite Sport
3. Sports in _____ (another country)
4. An Exciting Game
5. A Stubborn Person
6. A Big Disappointment
7. Wrestling
8. There's Too Much Acting in Professional Wrestling
9. The Importance of Exercise
10. He/She Refused to Quit
11. Winning Is the Most Important Thing
12. How You Play Is the Most Important Thing

IX. *Word Families*

Complete the sentence with the following words. If necessary, add an ending to the word so it forms a correct sentence. (adj. = adjective and adv. = adverb)

1. **stubborn** (adj.)   **stubbornly** (adv.)   **stubbornness** (noun)

   A. Oscar made a big mistake, but he _____ refused to admit it.

   B. Bonnie and I are good friends, but sometimes her _____ drives me crazy.

   C. Kim can't persuade her husband to go to the play with her. He's

   very _____ .

2. **to refuse**   **refusal** (noun)

   A. Mel wouldn't let me borrow his car. His _____ surprised me.

   B. The department store sent me a bill for clothing I didn't buy. Naturally

   I _____ to pay it.

3. **to soak**   **soaked** (adj.)

   A. You should _____ the paint brushes in turpentine.

   B. We can't play baseball today. It rained all night and the field is

   _____ .

4. **to disappoint**   **disappointment** (noun)   **disappointed** (adj.)
   disappointing (adj.)   **disappointingly** (adv.)

   A. The _____ student asked the teacher why his mark was so low.

   B. The crowd at the concert was _____ small.

   C. I'm sorry to _____ you, but I can't go to the beach with you tomorrow. I'm going to be away.

   D. Phil had a _____ day. Nothing went right at work.

   E. The party was a _____ . We didn't enjoy it.

41

X.   *Building Words with -al (-ial)*

The suffix **-al (-ial)** is added to nouns to form an adjective. The suffix **-al** means **having to do with**, for example, **financial** means **having to do with finance; professional** means **having to do with a profession.**

The suffix **-al (-ial)** is also added to verbs to form a noun. In this case, **-al** means **the act of**, for example, **arrival** means **the act of arriving; denial** means **the act of denying**.

Noun	*Adjective*
accident	accidental
addition	additional
culture	cultural
finance	financial
nation	national
nature	natural
norm	normal
occasion	occasional
origin	original
person	personal
practice	practical
profession	professional
race	racial
season	seasonal
tradition	traditional

Verb	*Noun*
arrive	arrival
deny	denial
refuse	refusal
survive	survival
try	trial

Complete the sentences with these words.

arrival	additional	denial	traditional
accidental	financial	original	professional

1. On Thanksgiving Day it's _____ to have turkey for dinner.

2. Gus didn't mean to shoot his friend. It was _____ .

3. I like Doctor Reyes. She's thorough and _____ .

4. Our company is having _____ problems. Profits are going down and expenses are rising.

5. Everyone is eagerly awaiting the President's _____ .

6. Cynthia was surprised by the bank's _____ of her loan.

7. The museum has several of Picasso's _____ paintings.

8. The tickets to the soccer game cost ten dollars, and there's an

   _____ fee for parking.

Five

Ray's Sweetheart

Preview Questions

Discuss or think about these questions before reading the story.

1. Dating often starts very young in the United States. How old should a girl and boy be before they begin dating, before they start going out alone?

2. What qualities do you think a girl looks for in a boyfriend? In other words, what makes a boy popular with girls?

3. What qualities does a boy look for in a girlfriend?

Ray's Sweetheart

Ray is not only an outstanding basketball player, but he's handsome and friendly. He's very popular with the girls. He has dated several of them, but Linda is his sweetheart. She goes to the same school as Ray and is also a basketball star. She's the captain of the girl's team. Ray goes to most of her games and she goes to most of his. She's crazy about him and he adores her. They go out quite often. Linda loves to dance and she's an excellent dancer. Ray takes her dancing most weekends. He's not the best dancer in the world, but he likes to dance too.

Linda is very smart and she's going to study to be a doctor. She's also very kind, but there's a **flaw** in her personality. She gets **jealous** easily. When she sees Ray talking with other girls, it makes her unhappy. She's especially unhappy when she sees him with Barbara. Ray used to go out with Barbara, but they don't date anymore. They're just friends now. However, Linda **suspects** that Ray is still interested in Barbara.

He knows that Linda is jealous and he **teases** her sometimes. He will **praise** Barbara and say she's a wonderful person. Linda tries to **hide** her feelings by smiling and agreeing with him, but she gets angry when he praises Barbara. Barbara knows all about Ray and Linda's friendship, but it doesn't bother her at all. "I have my own boyfriend," she says, "and I don't care who he goes out with. It's a free country."

The other night Ray and Linda went to the movies. Afterwards, they stopped at a diner to get something to eat. Their conversation was so interesting that they didn't notice how late it was. By the time Ray brought Linda home, it was one o'clock.

Linda took off her shoes and tried to **sneak** into her room, but her parents were still up. They would never go to bed before she got home. They're very strict with Linda, and they worry when she's late. They had told her to be home by midnight. They **scolded** her, and she said, "I'm sorry, but we didn't realize how late it was. It won't happen again." "It better not," her father replied, "or you won't be dating anyone for a month. Now get to bed."

I. Comprehension Questions

If the sentence is true, write T. If it's false, write F.

_____ 1. Ray is popular with the girls because he's smart.

_____ 2. Both Ray and Linda are outstanding athletes.

_____ 3. Linda is crazy about Ray, but he's not sure he loves her.

_____ 4. Linda wants to be a nurse or secretary.

_____ 5. She gets upset when other girls show a special interest in Ray.

_____ 6. He says nice things about Barbara to annoy Linda.

_____ 7. Barbara doesn't care if Ray dates other girls.

_____ 8. Ray took Linda home right after the movie.

_____ 9. She tried to get into her room as quietly as possible.

_____ 10. She told her parents that they worry too much.

II. MINI-DICTIONARY — PART ONE

---

1. **flaw** (flô) *noun:* defect; anything that makes a person or thing imperfect
   "No one is perfect. We all have **flaws**."

2. **jeal·ous** (jel′əs) *adjective:* upset because another is getting the love and attention one wants for oneself: upset because one does not have what another person has
   "Everyone pays so much attention to the new baby that it makes her sister **jealous**."

3. **sus·pect** (sə-spekt′) *verb:* to think something is true: to think someone has done something wrong
   (sus′pekt) *noun:* a person who is thought to have done something wrong
   "I **suspect** that Marina and Ivan will get married."
   "Mrs. Mason was shot last night and her husband is a **suspect**."

4. **tease** (tēz) *verb:* to say or do playfully to disturb someone: to cause someone to want something and then not allow the person to have it
   "I was just **teasing** when I said you're getting old."
   "Alex **teased** his brother by showing him the candy and not giving him any."

III.

Complete the sentences with these words. *If necessary, add an ending to the word so it becomes a correct sentence. Use each word twice.*

> tease   jealous   flaw   suspect

1. The police _____ that Bruce stole the money.

2. Marsha is very rich and her brothers are _____ .

3. I'm not going to buy that sweater. There's a _____ in it.

4. Never _____ a dog when he's eating.

5. Don gets _____ when his wife is friendly with other men.

6. Lucy is always _____ Frank. He usually likes it, but sometimes it annoys him.

7. No one knows who kidnapped Earl's son, and there are no

_____ .

8. There are some _____ in our plan.

IV.   MINI-DICTIONARY — PART TWO

5. **praise** (prāz) *verb:* to speak positively and warmly about a person or thing

    noun: positive and warm words about a person or thing

    "The director of the hospital frequently **praises** the nurses for their hard work and dedication."

    "Children need a lot of love and **praise**."

6. **hide** (hīd) *verb:* to keep secret: to put something where you hope others will not find it

    "I tried to **hide** my anger, but everyone knew I was annoyed."

    "Where can I **hide** this key?"

    The past tense of **hide** is **hid**.

7. **sneak** (snēk) *verb:* to move or act quietly and secretly so one will not be noticed

"Al tried to **sneak** into the game without paying."

> The past tense of **sneak** is **sneaked** or **snuck**.
> **Snuck** is informal, but it's used frequently and is now considered standard English.

8. **scold** (skōld) *verb*: to correct with anger
   "The police officer **scolded** me for speeding, but I didn't get a ticket."

V.

Complete the sentences with these words. *If necessary, add an ending to the word so it becomes a correct sentence. Use each word twice.*

> scold   hide   sneak   praise

1. In a recent speech, the President _____ the courage of the astronauts.

2. When Regina has a lot of cash at home, she _____ it in a shoebox.

3. Kristin isn't supposed to smoke, but sometimes she _____ a cigarette.

4. Did the teacher _____ you for coming late to class?

5. We didn't do anything wrong. We have nothing to _____ .

6. The new play won the _____ of the critics.

7. The doctor is going to _____ George. He has not been taking his medicine.

8. Doug's parents told him to stay home and study, but he _____ out of the house.

VI. *Preview Questions*

Discuss or think about these questions before completing the story.

1. What is the difference between an alcoholic and a person who sometimes gets drunk, but isn't an alcoholic?

2. Why do you think people become alcoholics?

3. Sometimes alcoholism runs in families. Why do you think this happens?

Complete the story with these words.

scolds	hide	flaw	praises
tease	sneaks	suspect	jealous

Lisa Drinks Too Much

Lisa is a history teacher at George Washington High School. She's one of the best teachers in the school. She's also the girl's basketball coach, and her team has won several championships. She's very popular with the students and gets along well with the other teachers, but a few of them are _____ of her success.

Lisa, however, has a problem. She loves to drink. Her friends used to _____ her about drinking so much, but they don't anymore because now they see that it's not just a little _____ ; it's a serious illness. Some of them _____ that she's an alcoholic and they're right.

When Lisa gets drunk, her husband _____ her. When she doesn't drink, he _____ her and she promises never to drink again. But when he's not around, she _____ a few drinks. Lisa realizes she's suffering from alcoholism and that she can't _____ her problem anymore. She has decided to go to Alcoholics Anonymous for help.

VII. Sharing Information

Discuss these questions in pairs or small groups.

A. Ray's Sweetheart

1. Do you like to dance? What are some of the dances or kinds of dancing you like? Are you a good dancer? Do you dance much?

2. What do you know about dating customs in other countries? Is there more supervision than in the United States? Does dating begin later?

3. Linda loves to play basketball. Do you think schools give girls as much opportunity to play sports as they do boys? If not, why not?

4. Jealously is a flaw. Name some other flaws people have.

5. Ray teases Linda. Do you ever tease anyone? Who? How? Does anyone tease you? Who? How?

6. Some teasing is good fun and some is cruel. Give an example of cruel teasing.

7. In the United States, April 1st is a special day for teasing. What is that day called? What do people do on that day?

8. How often do you go to the movies? Frequently? Sometimes? Almost never? Never? If you have a VCR, how often do you rent movies to watch at home?

B. Lisa Drinks Too Much

9. What is a hangover? What part of the body is often damaged by excessive drinking?

10. What are some of the other bad effects of drinking too much?

11. Many U.S. states have raised the age at which young people can be served or buy alcohol from eighteen to twenty-one. Why do you think they did this? Do you think the change was good or bad? Explain your answer.

12. What do you know about Alcoholics Anonymous? What are some of their ideas or principles? Do they have much success helping alcoholics?

13. Besides Alcoholics Anonymous, what other programs are there to help those suffering from alcoholism? Do you know of any in your community?

14. Lisa admits she's an alcoholic. Do you think people must admit they're alcoholic before they can be helped?

50

VIII. Topics for Writing or Speaking

Write a few lines, a paragraph, or a composition about one of these topics; or use them for further discussion or an oral report.

1. My Boyfriend/Girlfriend
2. My Best Friend
3. A Big Flaw
4. Jealousy
5. Teasing
6. A Movie I Liked
7. An Alcoholic Who Got Better
8. Alcoholics Anonymous
9. The Dangers of Drinking and Driving
10. The Drinking Age Should Be _____
11. There's Nothing Wrong with Having a Few Drinks
12. No One Should Drink

IX. Word Families

Complete the sentences with the following words. If necessary, add an ending to the word so it forms a correct sentence. (adj. = adjective and adv. = adverb)

1. **flaw** (noun)   **flawless** (adj.)   **flawlessly** (adv.)

   A. Stan played the piano ____flawlessly____.

   B. Leslie is checking the dress to make sure there are no ____flaw____ in the material.

   C. Everyone enjoyed the play. The acting was ____flawless____.

2. **jealous** (adj.)   **jealously** (adv.)   **jealousy** (noun)

   A. The cat ____jealously____ protected her kittens.

   B. ____Jealousy____ keeps people from enjoying what they have.

   C. My sister just brought a new Volvo and I'm ____jealous____.

3. **suspect** (verb or noun)   **suspicion** (noun)   **suspicious** (adjective) **suspiciously** (adv.)

   A. Don't be so ____suspicious____! No one is trying to harm you.

   B. Mary Lou has a terrible pain in her side. I ____suspect____ she has appendicitis. I'm taking her to the hospital.

   C. The police questioned Keith because he was acting ____suspiciously____.

D. Stacey has been living in the Soviet Union for three years, and I have a _____suspicion_____ she's working for the Central Intelligence Agency (C.I.A.).

4. **to sneak**   **sneaky** (adj.)   **sneakers** (noun)

A. Billy is _____sneaking_____ into the kitchen to get some cookies.

B. We have to wear _____sneakers_____ when we play in the gym.

C. No one trusts Margaret. She's _____sneaky_____ .

5. **to scold**   **scolding** (noun)

A. Grace gave her son a _____scolding_____ . He had hit his sister.

B. The librarian _____scolded_____ the students for making so much noise.

X. *Building Words with -ity (-ty, -y)*

The suffix **-ity (-ty, -y)** is added to adjectives to form a noun. This suffix means **the state or quality of being**, for example, **possibility** means **the state of being possible; loyalty** means **the quality of being loyal**.

Adjective	Noun
able	ability
active	activity
available	availability
brief	√brevity
common	community
curious	curiosity
difficult	difficulty
electric	electricity
honest	honesty
jealous	jealousy
loyal	loyalty
opportune	opportunity
original	originality
popular	popularity
possible	possibility
public	publicity
responsible	responsibility
sincere	sincerity

Complete the sentences with these words.

opportunity　　　**difficulty**　　　**honesty**　　　**community**
ability　　　　　**popularity**　　**electricity**　**responsibility**

1. I'm not going to clean your room. That's your _____ .

2. Brian is having _____ with his math homework. Can you help him?

3. Big cities are great to visit, but I prefer to live in a small _____ .

4. Audrey was just offered an excellent job. It's a wonderful _____ .

5. The mayor may not get reelected. His _____ is going down.

6. You need a lot of _____ to be a good doctor.

7. Chen is known for his _____ . He won't lie or steal.

8. Air conditioners are nice, but they use a great deal of _____ .

Six

Cheating on a Test

Preview Questions

Discuss or think about these questions before reading the story.

1. What can a teacher do to prevent students from cheating on a test, that is, from getting answers from other students?

2. What should a teacher do if she catches a student cheating on a test?

3. Why is it wrong to cheat on a test?

Cheating on a Test

Ray is one of the best students in his class. He's especially good in math and science. They're his favorite subjects and he always gets high marks in them. He knows he has to do well in them if he wants to be an engineer. He gets good grades in history and Spanish too, but he doesn't like these subjects as much and only studies them when he has a test.

Ray is a very honest person. He **would rather** do poorly on a test than look at another student's paper. However, he also likes to help people and wants to be popular with everyone. This got him into a lot of trouble yesterday.

He had a math test and his friend George asked for help during the test. Ray didn't want to **cheat** and at first he refused. But the **pressure** was too much for him. George is a good friend, and he hadn't studied for the test. Math is George's worst subject.

At the beginning of the test, Ray **whispered** some answers to George, but he was afraid the teacher would hear him. So he wrote the answers on a piece of paper and gave them to George. Just as he did this, the teacher **glanced** at Ray and saw what he was doing. The teacher had warned the class that anyone caught cheating would get a zero. So she took their tests and gave them both zero. This meant Ray would get an F on his next report card.

Ray knew he had to tell his parents what happened. He **dreaded** this. His parents were upset and disappointed. They told him he would have to learn to say no when asked to do something wrong. They told him he couldn't play basketball for two weeks. Ray thought this was a **harsh** punishment. The one thing he loves to do is to play basketball. He told his parents he **regretted** what he had done and wouldn't do it again. "That's good," they said, "but we still aren't going to let you play basketball for two weeks."

Ray's coach was unhappy about losing him in the middle of the season, and, of course, he was angry at Ray for cheating. He understood that Ray's parents had to punish him in some way. He only wished they hadn't made him stop playing basketball for two weeks.

I.   Comprehension Questions

Answer these questions about the story. *Use your judgment to answer questions with an asterisk. Work in pairs or small groups.* The number in parentheses indicates the paragraph in which the answer is found.

1. What special reason does Ray have for wanting to do well in math and science? (1) *want to be an engineer*
2. Why would Ray rather do poorly on a test than cheat? (2) *he is honest*
3. When George asked him to cheat, what did Ray do at first? (3) *he refuse to do it*
4. Why did he change his mind and give the answers to George? (3) *peer pressure*
5. How did he give George the answers at the beginning of the test? (4) *whisper*
6. What did the teacher do when she saw that they were cheating? (4) *give both of them a zero.*
*7. Do you think the teacher was too harsh in giving them zeros?
*8. If you were their teacher and caught them cheating, what would you have done?
9. What did Ray dread? (5)
10. How did his parents punish him? (5) *stop him to play basketball for two weeks.*
*11. Do you think his parents were too harsh in the way they punished him?
*12. If you were his mother or father, what would you have done?

II. *MINI-DICTIONARY — PART ONE*

1. **would rath·er** (wŏŏd ra*th*′er) *idiom:* to prefer; to like to do one thing more than another

   "Bert wants to stay home and watch TV. I **would rather** go to the movies."

2. **cheat** (chēt) *verb:* to act dishonestly or unfairly; to gain unfair advantage

   "We don't like to play cards with Cathy. We know she **cheats**."

3. **pres·sure** (presh′ər) *noun:* the act or result of pressing: an attempt to force or influence a person to do something: situation or difficulty that causes anxiety

   verb: to attempt to force or influence a person to do something

   "The parents are putting **pressure** on the board of education to build a new high school."

   "The government is **pressuring** the company to hire more minority workers."

4. **whis·per** ((h)wis′pər) *verb:* to speak in a low voice

   noun: words spoken in a low voice

56

"Herb **whispered** to his friend so no one else would hear."
"Vicky spoke to me in a **whisper**. She didn't want to wake the baby."

III.

scoop around

Complete the sentences with these words. *If necessary, add an ending to the word so it forms a correct sentence. Use each word twice.*

cheat	whisper	would rather	pressure

1. Helen is the president of the bank. It's a great job, but there's a lot of ___pressure___ .

2. The little boy is ___whispering___ in his mother's ear.

3. Carol and Dick want to make sandwiches and eat in the park, but the children ___would rather___ go to McDonald's.

4. The cashier didn't give me the correct change, but she wasn't trying to ___cheat___ . She made a mistake.

5. I ___would rather___ fly to Washington than take the train.

6. We wrote to our senators to ___pressure___ them to vote to increase our social security benefits..

7. Victor tried to ___cheat___ the government by not paying his taxes, but he got caught.

8. Why are you speaking in a ___whisper___ ? Is there something you don't want us to hear?

IV. *MINI-DICTIONARY — PART TWO*

---

5. **glance** (glans) *verb:* to look at quickly
   noun: a quick look
   "Sheila **glanced** at the children playing in the yard."
   "I took a quick **glance** at the ad and threw it away."

6. **dread** (dred) *verb:* to fear greatly, especially something in the future
   noun: great fear, especially of something in the future

57

"We **dreaded** telling Carmen that her husband was badly hurt in an auto accident."

"I enjoy school, but I have a **dread** of exams."

7. **harsh** (härsh) *adjective:* severe; very unpleasant

"Chicago has **harsh** winters."

8. **re·gret** (ri·gret′) *verb:* to feel sorry about: to wish you had not done something

noun: a feeling of sorrow: a wish you had not done something

"Len **regretted** that he couldn't help us."

"Julie's mother died. I sent her a card expressing our **regrets**."

V.

Complete the sentences with these words. *If necessary, add an ending to the word so it forms a correct sentence. Use each word twice.*

harsh	dread	glance	regret

1. Mi Chong lives in San Francisco, and she ____dreads____ the thought of another earthquake.

2. The company ____regrets____ that they have to close the factory.

3. Pedro ____glanced____ at the lake as he drove by.

4. Ellen's ____harsh____ criticism made us angry.

5. I ____dread____ driving in the snow.

6. The reporters asked the governor some ____harsh____ questions about the budget.

7. One ____glance____ and the doctor knew my son had the measles.

8. Since Brett is making more money, he has no ____regret____ about changing jobs.

58

VI. Preview Questions

Discuss or think about these questions before completing the story.

1. Many people think they will look and feel better if they lose weight. Do you want to lose weight, gain weight, or stay the same? *I want to lose weight.*

2. Why can it be dangerous to be overweight? *Overweight can cause lots of diseases, such as heart attack.*

3. Why is high blood pressure dangerous? *High blood pressure can cause persons to die or to paralyze.*

Complete the story with these words.

pressure	harsh	glanced	cheats
would rather	dreads	whispered	regrets

What Will the Doctor Say?

Steve Robinson is the principal of George Washington High School. He was meeting with some of the teachers when his secretary came into the room and _____*whispered*_____ to him. She was reminding him of his three o'clock appointment with Doctor Rutkowski. Steve _____*glanced*_____ at his watch and excused himself from the meeting. He _____*would rather*_____ get to the doctor's office a little early than be a minute late. He's an early bird.

Steven has high blood _____*pressure*_____, and last year he had a mild heart attack. The doctor put him on a low-sodium, low-fat diet, and told him to lose weight. Steve _____*regrets*_____ that he didn't follow the diet, but he loves salt and rich food and he often _____*cheats*_____ on his diet.

Steve has gained ten pounds and he _____*dreads*_____ seeing the doctor. He knows the doctor will have some _____*harsh*_____ words for him when he discovers that Steve has gained weight.

VII. Sharing Information

Discuss these questions in pairs or small groups.

A. Cheating on a Test

1. What was or is your favorite subject(s) in school?

2. Do you like math? Do you do well in math?

3. In what occupations is math especially important?

4. Do you like to study history? What is the value of studying history?

5. Pressure from friends often makes teenagers do things they shouldn't. Give some examples of this besides cheating.

6. Do you think most high-school and college students would cheat on a test if they weren't doing so well and thought they wouldn't get caught?

7. Cheating on a test is one example of cheating. Give some other examples.

B. What Will the Doctor Say?

8. Some people are almost always early. They're early birds. Others are just the opposite; they're usually late. Are you an "early bird" or a "late bird"?

9. The culture of some countries places a lot of importance on being on time. Is this true of the United States?

10. What do you know about your blood pressure? Is it high? Average? Low?

11. Eating too much salt can be dangerous, especially if you have high blood pressure. Do you like salt a lot? Do you put much on your food? Does the body need some salt?

12. A low-fat diet seems to lower the risk not only of a heart attack, but of certain types of cancer, for example, cancer of the colon. Name some low-fat foods. Name some high-fat foods.

VIII. Topics for Writing or Discussion

Write a few lines, a paragraph, or a composition about one of these topics; or use them for further discussion or an oral report.

1. My Favorite Subject
2. Why It's Important to Study History
3. Cheating
4. Something I Dread
5. A Harsh Punishment
6. Something I Regret
7. Why It's Important to Be on Time
8. An Early Bird/A Late Bird
9. An Excellent Doctor
10. The Best Way to Diet
11. How I Lost _____ Pounds
12. Some Diets Are Dangerous

IX. Word Families

Complete the sentences with the following words. If necessary, add an ending to the word so it forms a correct sentence. (adj. = adjective and adv. = adverb)

1. **pressure** (noun or verb)　　**to press**　　**pressing** (adj.)

   A. I ____pressed____ the button and the elevator came right away.

   B. Hal is an air-traffic controller, and he loves his job despite the ____pressure____ .　　*blimp*

   C. We're not going to buy a new car now. We have more ____pressing____ needs.

2. **dread** (verb or noun)　　**dreadful** (adj.)　　**dreadfully** (adv.)

   A. Washington, D.C., can be ____dreadfully____ hot and humid in the summer.

   B. Leona ____dreads____ thunder and lightning storms.
   io girl's name
   C. The plane crash was ____dreadful____ . Eighty passengers lost their lives.

3. **harsh** (adj.)　　**harshly** (adv.)　　**harshness** (noun)

   A. The teacher spoke ____harshly____ to the class. He was very angry.

   B. Because of the ____harshness____ of the climate, few people live in Alaska.

   C. The training and discipline in the army are ____harsh____ .

   bundle? up with coat

61

4. **regret** (verb or noun) **regretful*** (adj.) **regretfully** (adv.)
   regretttable* (adj.) **regrettably** (adv.)

   A. Prices keep going up. It's _____regrettable_____ , but there's not much
      we can do about it.
   B. The _____regretful_____ manager had to fire several workers.
   C. Sal was in an auto accident last night. _____Regrettably_____ , he had
      been drinking.
   D. Emily _____regretted_____ that she never finished high school.
   E. The doctor _____regretfully_____ told Mrs. Robinson that her baby was
      very sick.

Regretful means *feeling or showing regret*. **Regrettable** means *causing regret or deserving blame*. A
person who feels regret is **regretful**. An action that causes regret or deserves blame is **regrettable**.

X.

A. Synonyms

*Next to each sentence, write a **synonym** for the underlined word or phrase. If
necessary, add an ending to the synonym.*

flaw	regret	heal	dread
harsh	would rather	scold	jealous

1. I hurt my knee skiing, but it's getting better. _____heal_____
2. Sandra likes to cook, but she prefers to eat out. _____would rather_____
3. My brother's business is very successful and I'm a little envious.
   _____jealous_____ .
4. We inspected the furniture carefully to make sure there were no defects.
   _____flaws_____
5. Pam corrected her son for being fresh. _____scolded_____ that's fresh
   impolite = sassy
6. In the Middle East, the penalties for stealing are severe.
   _____harsh_____
7. Harry is afraid of going to the dentist. _____dread_____
8. I am sorry that I hurt your feelings. _____regret_____

If a man said something badly to you → "you are rude".
If girls say to boys "you are fresh"
that means that the boys' manners are too friendly and too soon.

62

B. Antonyms

*Using the words below, complete each sentence with an **antonym** of the underlined word. If necessary, add an ending to the antonym.*

hide	praise	stubborn	whisper
cheat	refuse	disappoint	outstanding

1. There's no need to <u>shout</u>. I can hear you even when you ___whisper___ .

2. If the economy does well, we ___praise___ the President. If it does poorly, we <u>blame</u> him.

3. Marissa is an <u>ordinary</u> skater, but her sister is ___outstanding___ .

4. Bruce is always <u>honest</u>. He never ___cheats___ .

5. Pam is <u>flexible</u>, but her mother is very ___stubborn___ .

6. Most of the students were <u>satisfied</u> with their grades, but a few were ___disappointed___ .

7. During my job interview, I <u>showed</u> my strengths and ___hid___ my weaknesses.

8. Gary <u>agreed</u> to vote for me, but his wife ___refused___ .

XI. Building Words with mis-

The prefix **mis-** is placed in front of nouns and verbs. **Mis-** means (a) **bad** or **badly**, for example, **misfortune** means **bad fortune** and **misbehave** means **to behave badly**: (b) **incorrect** or **incorrectly**, for example, **misprint** means **incorrect printing** and **mispronounce** means **to pronounce incorrectly**: (c) **a lack of**, for example, **mistrust** means **a lack of trust**.

Verb or *Noun*	*Verb* or *Noun*
behave	misbehave
fortune	misfortune
inform	misinform
interpret	misinterpret
judge	misjudge
lead	mislead
place	misplace

63

Verb or *Noun*	*Verb* or *Noun*
print	misprint
pronounce	mispronounce
represent	misrepresent
spell	misspell
take	mistake
treat	mistreat
trust	mistrust
understand	misunderstand
use	misuse

Complete the sentences with these words.

mistreats	**misfortune**	**misbehave**	**misled**
misprints	**misplaced**	**mistrust**	**misunderstood**

1. Janet punishes her children when they ___misbehave___ .

2. You ___misunderstood___ what I said. Let me explain.

3. There are some ___misprints___ in this book.

4. I think Fred lies a lot. That's why I ___mistrust___ him.   *lack of trust*

5. Sally had the ___misfortune___ of buying a new car with several defects.

6. Sometimes Gary ___mistreats___ his dog. That's cruel.

7. I ___misplaced___ my wallet. Did you see it?

8. The ad in the newspaper ___misled___ a lot of people.

Unit Three
A Young Family

Seven

A Joy and a Burden

Preview Questions

Discuss or think about these questions before reading the story.

1. For most mothers, taking care of a baby is both a joy and a burden. Why?

2. What are some of a baby's physical needs?

3. What are some of a baby's psychological needs? read, rock, soothe

4. How do babies get on our nerves?

get you angry

A Joy and a Burden

My name is Kim and I married Chris Johnson four years ago. That was a great day, but the happiest day of my life was the day our son was born. His name is David, and I want to tell you all about him. He's ten months old and he weighs twenty pounds. I think he's the cutest baby in the world; I adore him.

David is too young to walk, but he can **crawl**, and he loves to crawl across the living room rug. He's also just beginning to talk and I talk to him a lot. He understands most of the things I say and he can say a few words himself, like "Da-Da" and "Mommy."

David gets cranky[1] when he's tired, but he's in a good **mood** most of the time. I love it when he smiles or laughs. Sometimes I **tickle** him just to see him laugh.

Taking care of David is a joy, but it's also a **burden**. David is so active and curious. I know this helps him **develop**, but it also gets him into trouble and gives me gray hair. Let me give you an example.

Yesterday David was playing in the living room, and I was sitting on the sofa and sewing buttons on a blouse. I didn't realize it, but a large button had fallen on the floor. David picked it up and put it in his mouth. Fortunately, I saw what he had done. I quickly took the button out of his mouth and told him never to do that again. He could have **choked** on the button. I have to watch David all the time. He **grabs** everything he can reach, and if it's small enough, he puts it in his mouth.

The only time during the day that I get a break is when David takes his afternoon nap. If I'm lucky, he sleeps for two hours. This gives me a chance to get some things done around the house. But sometimes I just sit and read a book or magazine, and enjoy the peace and quiet. Every once in a while, I **peek** at David to make sure he's okay.

My biggest problem with David is that he doesn't like to go to sleep at night. Most babies his age are asleep by eight o'clock, but not David. I call him "The Owl."[2] I rock him until he's almost asleep and then I put him in his crib. As soon as his head hits the pillow, he starts to cry. I pick him up, which is probably a mistake, and I rock him some more until he's sound asleep.

I love being a mother, but it's not an easy job. By the end of the day I'm exhausted.[3]

1. **Cranky** means *easily upset or angered*. Crying

2. An **owl** is a bird that is known for staying awake at night.

3. **Exhausted** means *extremely tired*.

rock the baby = rock in the arms.

67

I. Comprehension Questions

If the sentence is true, write T. If it's false, write F.

__F__ 1. Kim's wedding day was the happiest day of her life.

__T__ 2. David is only ten months old, but he can say a few words.

__F__ 3. He is always in a good mood.

__T__ 4. His curiosity gets him into trouble.

__F__ 5. Kim didn't see David put the button in his mouth.

__F__ 6. He swallowed the button.

__T__ 7. Kim likes David to take a long nap.

__T__ 8. While he naps, she reads or does housework.

__F__ 9. At night, David falls asleep easily.

__T__ 10. Kim has a tough job.

II. MINI-DICTIONARY — PART ONE

---

1. **crawl** (krôl) *verb:* to move on one's hands and knees: to move slowly

   noun: the act of moving on one's hands and knees: the act of moving slowly

   "The children are **crawling** under the fence to get into the yard."

   "The traffic on the highway slowed to a **crawl**."

2. **mood** (mo͞od) *noun:* the state of one's feelings

   "I don't know what's wrong, but Heather is in a bad **mood**."

3. **tick·le** (tik′əl) *verb:* to touch lightly to make one laugh

   "If you **tickle** Roy's feet, he'll laugh."

4. **bur·den** (bur′dən) *noun:* something hard to bear or do; a difficult task

   verb: to give a difficult task to; to give too much work to

68

"Keeping the house clean is a **burden**."
"The secretaries are very busy. Please don't **burden** them with more typing."

III.

Complete the sentences with these words. *If necessary, add an ending to the word so it forms a correct sentence. Use each word twice.*

| crawl | burden | mood | tickle |

1. Paying taxes is a ___burden___ .
2. I didn't like it when Edith ___tickled___ me with a feather.
3. Sid ___crawled___ under the table to get his pen.
4. Now is the time to ask the boss for a raise. She's in a great ___mood___ .
5. Yesterday I fell asleep in class, but my friend woke me up by ___tickling___ me.
6. We don't want to ___burden___ you, but we need your help.
7. This rainy weather doesn't help my ___moods___ .
8. The entrance to the cave was so low we had to ___crawl___ into it.

IV. MINI-DICTIONARY — PART TWO

---

5. **de·vel·op** (di·vel′əp) *verb:* to grow; to increase; to become more complete

   "A big storm is **developing** off the coast. We're going to get a lot of snow."

6. **choke** (chōk) *verb:* to have difficulty breathing or to stop breathing because the flow of air to the lungs is blocked: to cause someone to stop breathing by blocking the flow of air to the lungs

   "Cindy almost **choked** on a chicken bone."

7. **grab** (grab) *verb:* to take quickly and roughly; to take quickly
   "Tim **grabbed** his coat and left for work."

8. **peek** (pēk) *verb:* to look at quickly; to look at quickly and secretly
   noun: a quick look; a quick and secret look
   "Sue **peeked** in the oven to see if the cake was done."
   "I took a **peek** at the letter on Mario's desk."

V.

Complete the sentences with these words. *If necessary, add an ending to the word so it forms a correct sentence. Use each word twice.*

peek	**develop**	**grab**	**choke**

1. Allyson almost fell, but I _____grabbed_____ her arm just in time.
2. This part of the city is _____developing_____ fast.
3. Lynn can't breathe. She's _____choke_____ !
4. Gene _____peeked_____ at my paper during yesterday's exam.
5. Let's _____grab_____ something to eat before we go.
6. I didn't have time to read the magazine, but I took a _____peek_____ at the pictures.
7. Pablo jogs and rides a bike to _____develop_____ his leg muscles.
8. Help Angela quickly! She's _____choking_____ on some food.

VI. Preview Questions

Discuss or think about these questions before completing the story.

1. Do you have a smoke alarm(s) in your house or apartment? If you do, where is it?

2. Why are smoke alarms so important?

3. Are they expensive? Are they easy to install?

4. Does your state have a law that there must be smoke alarms in all motels, hotels, and apartment buildings?

70

Complete the story with these words.

peeked	burden	crawled	developed
choke	tickling	mood	grabbed

A Fire in the Motel

Karen and Ahmed are married and own a motel on Route 40 just outside of Saint Louis. The area has ___developed___ rapidly, and the motel makes a lot of money, but running it is a ___burden___. There are bills to pay, rooms to clean, and people to keep happy; and you never know when there's going to be an emergency.

Last year there was a fire in the motel. Ahmed was asleep in his room on the third floor when he heard the smoke alarm. He opened his door a crack and ___peek___ into the hall. It was full of smoke. Ahmed ___grabbed___ his flashlight and left the room.

The smoke was very thick and he started to ___choke___. Fortunately there was some fresh air close to the floor. Ahmed ___crawled___ to the exit and got out of the motel safely. Several people were hurt in the fire, but none seriously. However, the smoke did a lot of damage.

The fire and the problems of fixing the motel put Ahmed in a bad ___moool___. Karen wanted to cheer him up, so she tried to make him laugh by ___tickling___ his side, but he didn't think it was funny so she stopped. A few weeks later Ahmed felt much better, and now the motel is doing fine.

VII. Sharing Information

Discuss these questions in pairs or small groups.

A. A Joy and a Burden

1. Sometimes we're in a good mood and sometimes we're in a bad mood. Name some things that help put you in a good mood.

2. Name some things than can put you in a bad mood.

3. Babies are very curious and they love to touch things. Why is this good? What are some things we don't want them to touch?

4. David almost choked on a button. What are some other objects a baby can choke on?

5. What are some poisonous substances we should keep out of reach of babies?

6. When David is put to bed and starts to cry, Kim picks him up. Why is this probably a mistake?

7. It's common to hear mothers carry on "conversations" with babies and ask them questions long before they can speak. Why is this good for their speech development?

B. A Fire in the Motel

8. What are some things a motel manager must do or hire others to do?

9. When you go to a motel or hotel, do you check to make sure you know the best way out of the building in case of a fire? Why should you?

10. Is it okay to use an elevator if there is a fire? Why not?

11. What are some of the causes of fires in houses and motels?

12. In a hot, smoke-filled room or hall why is the best air close to the ground?

VIII. Topics for Writing or Speaking

Write a few lines, a paragraph, or a composition about one of these topics; or use them for further discussion or an oral report.

1. My Changing Moods
2. My Baby
3. A Baby
4. My Experience as a Babysitter
5. Why We Had to Rush the Baby to the Doctor/Hospital
6. The Psychological Needs of a Baby
7. Managing a Motel/Hotel
8. The Motel/Hotel We Stayed at
9. A Bad Fire
10. Rescued from a Fire
11. A Firefighter
12. Smoke Alarms

IX. Word Families

Complete the sentences with the following words. If necessary, add an ending to the word so it forms a correct sentence. (adj. = adjective and adv. = adverb)

1. **mood** (noun)   **moody** (adj.)   **moodiness** (noun)

   A. Tania is _____moody_____ . One minute she feels fine. The next minute she's very unhappy.

   B. I was in a great _____mood_____ until I saw the dentist's bill.

   *C. Wayne's _{ moodiness / mood }_____ makes him difficult to work with.

   *There are two possible answers to C.

2. **to tickle**   **ticklish** (adj.)

   Stephanie is very _____ticklish_____ . She can't help laughing when I _____tickle_____ her.

3. **burden** (noun or verb)   **burdensome** (adj.)

   A. Cutting the grass is _____burdensome_____ .

   B. Paying the mortgage every month is a big _____burden_____ .

73

4. **to develop   developer** (noun)   **development** (noun)
   developmental (adj.)

A. Juan is a real-estate ___developer___ . His company has built many houses and condos.

B. Alice took her son to a psychologist. He's having some ___developmental___ problems.

C. It took many years for the forest to ___develop___ .

D. Japanese businesses spend a lot of money on research and ___development___ .

X. *Building Words with -ish*

The suffix **-ish** is added to nouns and adjectives and forms an adjective. It means (a) **belonging to, of**, for example, **Spanish** means **of Spain**: (b) **having the qualities of, like a**, for example, **childish** means **like a child**: (c) **devoted to**, for example, **bookish** means **devoted to books**: (d) **to some degree, somewhat**, for example, **bluish** means **somewhat blue**.

Noun or *Adjective*	*Adjective*
blue, red, etc.	bluish, reddish, etc.
book	bookish
boy	boyish
child	childish
fool	foolish
girl	girlish
self	selfish
sheep	sheepish
slave	slavish
style	stylish
tickle	ticklish
young	youngish
England	English
Ireland	Irish
Jew	Jewish
Poland	Polish
Spain	Spanish
Sweden	Swedish
Turkey	Turkish

74

Complete the sentences with these words.

girlish	bookish	slavish	Polish
Jewish	foolish	stylish	selfish

1. Kathy is _____selfish_____ . She never wants to share.
2. Howie is always reading. He's _____bookish_____ .
3. You're _____foolish_____ to stay in the sun so long.
4. Krystyna speaks _____Polish_____ .
5. Your dress is very _____stylish_____ . I like it.
6. Denise is on a diet. She wants to keep her _____girlish_____ figure.
7. Ernie has a _____slavish_____ devotion to his company. He does whatever the company asks.
8. On Saturday my friend goes to the synagogue. He's _____Jewish_____ .

Eight

A Job and the Threat of a Strike

Preview Questions

Discuss or think about these questions before reading the story.

1. Many students drop out of school, especially in our large cities. Why?

2. What can schools and parents do to help students stay in school?

3. What problems does this large dropout rate cause?

4. Why is it usually difficult for dropouts to find a job?

A Job and the Threat of a Strike

Chris Johnson met Kim when they were both still in high school. Chris was not much of a student. He liked his science class, but he thought all his other classes were boring. His parents and high-school guidance counselor tried to persuade him to finish high school, but he dropped out at the end of his junior year.[1] After he quit school, he got a job mowing lawns[2] for a landscape company. He liked this kind of work, but it was only for the summer.

In the fall, he started **seeking** a permanent job, but one was tough to find. He didn't have a high-school diploma, and he had no special skills and no experience. All the good jobs required experience or a skill.

Chris was getting discouraged. Things got so bad that he took a job at McDonald's. They paid him the minimum wage and he hated his work, but he didn't want to go back to high school, and he had to do something. So he worked at McDonald's and kept looking for a better job. He also went to an adult school two nights a week and earned his high-school equivalency diploma.

After working at McDonald's for six months, he got a job in a General Motors' plant in Detroit. He's been working there for eight years. His salary and fringe[3] benefits are excellent. He gets a month's vacation, free health care for himself and his family, and has a good pension plan.

The contract between General Motors and the auto workers **expires** at the end of the month. The union is seeking a pay **hike** of twelve percent a year, but they are willing to settle for seven percent. General Motors offered four. The union quickly **rejected** the offer and hopes for an early settlement **faded**.

The union and the company are **negotiating** to close the **gap** between the workers' demands and the company's offer. The **negotiators** meet every day, and both sides are eager to **avert** a strike. If there is one, both the workers and General Motors will lose money. In addition, competition from foreign cars, especially from Japan, makes a long strike unthinkable. But the workers are threatening to walk out if an agreement isn't reached by Monday.

Of course, Chris doesn't want a strike. "I have a wife and baby," he explains, "and we need all the money I bring home. If there's a strike, I'll get some money from the union, but it won't be as much as I get from General Motors."

1. The four years of high school are called freshman (first) year, sophomore (second) year, junior (third) year, and senior (fourth) year.

2. **Mow** means *to cut.* A **lawn** is *the grass around a house.*

3. **Fringe** means *extra* or *on the edge.* Vacations, health insurance, and pensions are examples of fringe benefits.

I. Comprehension Questions

Answer these questions about the story. *Use your judgment to answer questions with an asterisk. Work in pairs or small groups.* The number in parentheses indicates the paragraph in which the answer is found.

1. What class did Chris like? What did he think of his other classes? (1)

*2. What do you think Chris's parents said to try to persuade him to finish high school?

3. Why was it tough for Chris to find a good job? Give three reasons. (2)

4. What kind of salary did McDonald's pay Chris? (3)

*5. Why do you think he hated the work at McDonald's?

6. Name three fringe benefits he gets from General Motors. (4)

7. How big a raise is the union seeking and what did General Motors offer? (5)

8. How did the union react to General Motors' offer? (5)

*9. Why is the union asking for a twelve percent raise when they're willing to settle for seven?

10. Why are the workers and General Motors eager to avert a strike? (6)

*11. Why does foreign competition make a long strike unthinkable?

12. How will Chris support his family if there is a strike? (7)

II. MINI-DICTIONARY — PART ONE

1. **ex·pire** (ik·spīr') *verb:* to come to an end: to die
   "My Visa credit card **expires** next month."

2. **seek** (sēk) *verb:* to look for; to try to get
   "Columbus was **seeking** a new route to India when he discovered America."
   The past tense of **seek** is **sought**.

3. **hike*** (hīk) *noun:* increase; raise
   verb: to increase; to raise
   "Everyone in our building is unhappy about the rent **hike**."
   "Toyota is going to **hike** its prices soon."

   ***Hike** also means *a long walk, especially for pleasure and exercise.*

4. **re·ject** (ri·jekt′) *verb:* to refuse to accept; to say no to an offer
   (rē′jekt) *noun:* a person or thing that has been rejected
   "Gladys applied to Columbia University, but they **rejected** her."
   "The toy factory gives away its **rejects**, that is, the toys that don't pass inspection."

III.

Complete the sentences with these words. *If necessary, add an ending to the word so it forms a correct sentence. Use each word twice.*

seek   reject   expire   hike

1. When does your driver's license ___expire___ ?
2. The college announced a tuition ___hike___ for the fall term.
3. We want our club to grow so we're ___seeking___ new members.
4. My request for a transfer to another department was ___rejected___ .
5. The phone company plans to ___hike___ their rates.
6. Perry had a heart attack and ___expired___ before we could get a doctor.
7. The army accepted most applicants, but there were some ___rejects___ .
8. We should ___seek___ the truth.

IV.   *MINI-DICTIONARY — PART TWO*

5. **fade** (fād) *verb:* to slowly disappear: to lose color or strength
   "My red dress is old and it's beginning to **fade**."

6. **ne·go·ti·ate** (ni·gō′shē·āt′) *verb:* to talk with a person or group about some difference to try to come to an agreement
   ne·go·ti·a·tor (ni·gō′shē·ā`tər) *noun:* a person who negotiates
   "Mr. Rodriguez wants to sell his house and I want to buy it. We are **negotiating** the price."
   "The **negotiators** from the Soviet Union and the United States are meeting in Geneva."

7. **a·vert** (ə·vûrt′) *verb:* to keep something from happening; to prevent
   "Eric stopped his car just in time to **avert** an accident."

8. **gap** (gap) *noun:* separation: difference: empty space
   "There is a **gap** in the fence."

V.

Complete the sentences with these words. *If necessary, add an ending to the word so it forms a correct sentence. Use each word twice.*

gap	negotiate	avert	fade

1. Exercise and a low-fat diet help to _____ *avert* _____ heart attacks.

2. Robin is a lawyer, and she is _____ *negotiating* _____ for her client.

3. The war went on and hope for peace _____ *faded* _____ .

4. There is a _____ *gap* _____ between the mountains.

5. The firefighters and city recently _____ *negotiate* _____ a new contract.

6. The police arrived and _____ *negotiated* _____ a fight between the gangs.

7. Phyllis knows a lot about American history, but there are some

   _____ *gaps* _____ in her knowledge.

8. The flowers are _____ *fading* _____ . I'm throwing them out.

VI. Preview Questions

Discuss or think about these questions before completing the story.

The U.S. government usually spends more money than it collects. Many years the deficit has been large. As a result, the United States has a huge national debt.

1. Do you think the government should cut spending to balance the budget?

2. Or do you think that the government should continue the programs it has and raise taxes to balance the budget?

3. Or do you think the government should cut spending *and* raise taxes to balance the budget?

Complete the story with these words.

hike	fading	avert	seeking
reject	gap	expires	negotiating

The National Budget

In Washington, D.C., Congress[1] is preparing the budget for the coming year. The problem is that there is a large _____gap_____ between the amount of money the government will collect and the amount it plans to spend. Congress hopes to cut the budget, but there is no way they can _____avert_____ a deficit this year.

The House of Representatives is working on the budget this week. A few representatives want a tax _____hike_____, but the President and most representatives _____reject_____ that idea. A representative's term in office _____expires_____ after two years, and most of them are _____seeking_____ reelection this November. Naturally, these representatives are reluctant to raise taxes or cut spending.

The President has threatened to veto[2] the budget if Congress doesn't cut spending and reduce the deficit. Congress and the White House are _____negotiating_____ the spending cuts, but hopes for a quick agreement are _____fading_____.

1. Congress consists of the Senate and the House of Representatives. Members of the House of Representatives are called congressmen or congresswomen, and they have two-year terms. Senators have six-year terms.

2. The President has the power to *veto,* that is, to reject any bill passed by Congress, but Congress can override the veto if two-thirds of the Senate and House vote to do so.

VII. Sharing Information

Discuss these questions in pairs or small groups.

A. A Job and the Threat of a Strike

1. Some students say they drop out of school because it's boring. Do you think school is boring?

2. Some classes are boring. What makes a class boring?

3. What can a teacher do to make a class interesting?

4. What is a high-school equivalency diploma? What do you have to do to get one?

5. Name some jobs that don't require much skill or much education. Do any of them pay well?

6. The government sets a minimum wage, the least amount an employer can pay per hour. What is the minimum wage now? What are the benefits of having a minimum wage? What problems can it cause?

7. Auto workers in the United States get good salaries. If their salaries go much higher, they risk losing their jobs. Why?

8. If you're working, what fringe benefits do you receive? Health insurance? Vacation? Sick days? Pension? Life insurance? Dental plan? Eyeglass plan? Prescription plan? Other benefits?

B. The National Debt

9. What are some of the disadvantages of having such a large national debt?

10. Why is it difficult to raise taxes in an election year? Why is it difficult to cut spending in an election year?

11. Each state has two senators. Can you name the two senators from your state? Can you name the member of the House of Representatives from your congressional district?

12. Why is it important for all eligible citizens to vote? If you're eighteen and a citizen, are you registered to vote?

VIII. Topics for Writing or Speaking

Write a few lines, a paragraph, or a composition about one of these topics; or use them for further discussion or an oral report.

1. School Is Interesting/Boring
2. An Interesting/Boring Class
3. Why Students Drop Out
4. Fringe Benefits
5. A Job I Didn't Like
6. The House of Representatives/A Congressman/Congresswoman
7. The Senate/A Senator
8. Why It's Important to Vote
9. Our National Debt
10. Why and How We Should Cut Spending
11. Why and How We Should Raise Taxes

IX. Word Families

Complete the sentences with the following words. If necessary, add an ending to the word so it forms a correct sentence. (adj. = adjective and adv. = adverb)

1. **to expire   expiration** (noun)

   A. What's the _____expiration_____ date on your visa?

   B. My subscription to *Time* magazine _____expires_____ this month; I'm going to renew it.

2. **reject** (verb or noun)   **rejection** (noun)

   A. The prisoner's request for parole was _____rejected_____ by the parole board.

   B. Stella applied for a job and received a letter of _____rejection_____ this morning. She's very upset.

3. **to negotiate   negotiation** (noun)   **negotiable** (adjective)

   A. Lengthy _____negotiations_____ between the United States and Japan have solved some of our trade problems.

   B. Most items in the contract are _____negotiable_____, but a few are not.

   C. You can _____negotiate_____ in some jewelry stores; others have fixed prices.

4. **to avert**   **aversion** (noun)   **averse** (adj.)

A. Caroline doesn't like to cook. She won't be _____ to eating out.

B. The Alaskan oil spill could have been _____ .

C. My cousin is lazy. He has an _____ to work.

X.   *Building Words with -ize*

The suffix **-ize** is added to adjectives and nouns and forms a verb. The suffix **-ize** often means **to make**, for example, **legalize** means **to make legal**; **modernize** means **to make modern**. The form **-ise** is sometimes used instead of **-ize**, especially in British English.

Noun or *Adjective*	*Verb*
analysis	analyze
critic	criticize
emphasis	emphasize
final	finalize
general	generalize
hospital	hospitalize
legal	legalize
liberal	liberalize
maximum	maximize
memory	memorize
minimum	minimize
modern	modernize
public	publicize
real	realize
summary	summarize

Complete the sentences with these words.

hospitalized	legalize	emphasized	maximize
modernize	minimize	criticize	memorize

1. Mimi wants to _____ her kitchen.

2. Do you think the government should _____ betting?

3. Businesses like to _____ profits and _____ expenses.

4. The history teacher told us we would have to _____ some important dates.

5. The nurse _____ the importance of a balanced diet.

6. It was a bad accident. The driver was _____ .

7. I get angry when people _____ me.

Nine

A Good Husband with Some Bad Habits

Preview Questions

Discuss or think about these questions before reading the story.

1. Are women naturally better than men at taking care of babies? Explain your answer.

2. Who usually cares for newborn animals, their mother or father?

3. Today, fathers are more active in taking care of their babies than before. Is this good for the baby? Why?

4. Is this good for the father? Why? Is it good for the mother? Why?

A Good Husband with Some Bad Habits

Kim is a real-estate agent, and she worked full-time until David, her baby, was born. Now she works on the weekends when her husband Chris can take care of David.

Kim decided to return to work for several reasons, but the biggest was money. Chris's salary covered their everyday expenses, but left nothing to **spare** for emergencies. When Kim and Chris discovered a **leak** in their roof and were told it would cost six thousand dollars for a new one, Chris realized it would help a lot if his wife went back to work part-time.

Money, however, wasn't the only reason Kim returned to work. She enjoys getting away from the house and its **chores**. She likes to meet and work with people, and she's proud of her ability to sell houses.

Kim works every Saturday from nine to five. This means that Chris has to take care of David for eight hours. That was quite a challenge for Chris. He had never changed or fed a baby in his life. The first time he held David he was afraid he would drop him. When Chris was growing up, taking care of babies was a woman's job. But times are changing and so is Chris.

When the weather is nice, Chris likes to take the baby into the backyard. David has a sandbox there, and he loves to **dig** in it. Chris put the sandbox under a big oak tree so the baby could play in the **shade**, and he could sit in it. Sometimes Bruno, his nextdoor neighbor, will come over and chat with Chris. They like to talk about sports and to **gossip** a little.

The first few weekends that Chris watched David, he couldn't wait until his wife got home from work, but now he doesn't **mind** watching him. Chris always loved his baby a lot, but taking care of him every weekend has brought them even closer.

Kim is delighted that Chris is doing so well taking care of David, but he has a flaw that gets on her nerves. He is "Mr. Forgetful." He forgets to turn off the lights when he leaves a room, and he leaves his dirty clothes on the floor instead of putting them in the hamper.[1] He forgets to hang up his coat and frequently leaves empty soda glasses in the living room. One day Kim found a box of cereal in the refrigerator.

Kim **nags** him about these things, but it doesn't help at all. "When I first got married, I was so naive[2] I thought I could change Chris, but now I know better," she says. "Maybe I'm lucky. Chris doesn't drink, smoke, or gamble. Being forgetful isn't the worst fault in the world."

1. A **hamper** is *a basket with a lid.* It is used to store laundry, especially dirty laundry.

2. To be **naive** means *to believe too easily because of a lack of experience and knowledge.*

I. *Comprehension Questions*

If the sentence is true, write T. If it's false, write F.

_____ 1. Kim used to work full-time selling houses.

_____ 2. Chris takes care of David on the weekends.

_____ 3. Kim returned to work mostly because she wanted a career.

_____ 4. Chris repaired the leak in the roof.

_____ 5. It was easy for Chris to take care of David.

_____ 6. Chris wanted David to play in the sun.

_____ 7. Chris and Bruno like to discuss sports and to talk about other people.

_____ 8. Chris feels closer to his son than before.

_____ 9. Chris has a fault that annoys Kim.

_____ 10. Her nagging has changed Chris.

II. *MINI-DICTIONARY — PART ONE*

1. **spare** (spâr) *verb:* to give from what one has: to not punish or destroy
   adjective: extra
   "Can you **spare** a dollar?"
   "I said to the thief, 'Take my watch and wallet, but **spare** my life.' "
   "Rob can stay overnight at our house. We have a **spare** room."

2. **leak** (lēk) *noun:* a hole through which a gas or liquid accidentally goes out or comes in
   verb: to allow a gas or liquid to accidentally go out or come in through a hole
   "There's water on the kitchen floor. It's coming from a **leak** in the pipe under the sink."
   "The balloon won't hold air. It's **leaking**."

3. **chore** (chôr) *noun:* a routine task; a small unpleasant job
   "Washing clothes is a **chore**."

4. **dig** (dig) *verb:* to remove earth or sand, usually with a shovel
   "It'll be easy to **dig** here. The ground is soft."
   The past tense of **dig** is **dug**.

III.

Complete the sentences with these words. *If necessary, add an ending to the word so it forms a correct sentence. Use each word twice.*

leak	dig	chore	spare

1. Finish your _____ before you go out to play.

2. We have a _____ in our gas tank.

3. Can you _____ fifteen minutes to help me with my homework?

4. Jack is _____ in his yard. He's planting a tree.

5. Do you have any _____ change? I need a dime for the parking meter.

6. Milk is _____ from the grocery bag. There must be a hole in the milk carton.

7. Sometimes shopping is a _____ , and sometimes it's fun.

8. The workers are _____ for gold.

IV. *MINI-DICTIONARY — PART TWO*

5. **shade** (shād) *noun:* slight darkness caused by blocking the rays of
   the sun
   "The sun is hot. Let's sit in the **shade**."

6. **gos·sip** (gos'əp) *verb:* to talk about the private lives and actions of
   others
   noun: talk about the private lives and actions of
   others
   "Terry and Lee **gossip** a lot about their neighbors."
   "Did you hear the latest **gossip** about the mayor?"

7. **mind** (mīnd) *verb:* to dislike; to be disturbed by
   "Do you **mind** if I smoke?"
   "We don't **mind** waiting a few minutes."
   > **Mind** is used most often in questions and negative statements.

8. **nag** (nag) *verb:* to try to get a person to do something by suggesting, correcting, or complaining a lot
   "Vince **nags** his wife and she **nags** him."

V.

Complete the sentences with these words. *If necessary, add an ending to the word so it forms a correct sentence. Use each word twice.*

shade   mind   gossip   nag

1. Rose doesn't like her boss. He _____ her too much.

2. I don't _____ doing the dishes.

3. It's much cooler in the _____ .

4. Natalie frequently phones her friends. They talk about their children and their problems, and they _____ .

5. Do you _____ if I turn on the radio? I want to listen to some music.

6. The swimming pool is nice, but it doesn't have any _____ .

7. We don't know if it's true, but the _____ is that Fred has a new girlfriend.

8. I'm tired of your _____ . Please keep quiet.

VI. Preview Questions

Discuss or think about these questions before completing the story.

1. Do beauticians make good money?

2. Why do people tip beauticians and barbers?

3. Who else do we usually tip?

4. How do you feel about tipping? Are you for or against it?

Complete the story with these words.

chores	mind	dig	nag
leak	spare	gossip	shade

Busy Parents

Mark and Melissa are married and have two children. Melissa is a beautician and she loves her job. She works long hours, especially on Saturdays, but she doesn't _____ . She gets good tips, and she likes to _____ with her customers.

If Melissa weren't working, it would be difficult for the family to make ends meet.* They have a big mortgage and a lot of other bills, and they save all they can _____ so their children will be able to go to college.

Since Melissa is so busy, Mark, Melissa, and the children share the household _____ . Mark is good about helping around the house, but the children aren't. Mark and Melissa have to _____ them, or they won't do anything. They're teenagers and their favorite activity is talking on the phone.

Mark works for the Union Gas Company. He's a repairman and it's a tough job. Yesterday was especially difficult. There was a big gas _____ in the center of the city. Mark and two other repairmen had to _____ up the street. It was hot and sunny, and there was no _____

where they were working. Mark was tired when he got home.

*To make ends meet** is an idiom. It means *to have enough money to pay your bills.*

VII. *Sharing Information*

Discuss these questions in pairs or small groups.

A. A Good Husband with Some Bad Habits

1. A number of married women with children prefer part-time work. What part-time jobs are usually available? Do part-time workers usually get fringe benefits?

2. In general, who do you think gossips more, men or women? Explain your answer.

3. Are you good at putting things where they belong and turning out lights? Or are you a little forgetful like Chris?

4. Does anyone nag you? Who? Why?

5. Do you nag anyone? Who? Why?

6. Do you think most newlyweds feel they can change their spouses' bad habits? If so, is that realistic?

7. Does marriage change one's personality? Explain your answer.

8. In what ways is marriage likely to change a person?

B. Busy Parents

9. Why is it important that children do their share of the household chores? If you have children, what chores do they do?

10. Who does most of the housework where you live?

11. Why is it dangerous to be a repairperson for a gas company? Does that type of work pay well?

12. Why is it dangerous to stay long in the sun? What should a person do to lessen the danger?

VIII. Topics for Writing or Discussion

Write a few lines, a paragraph, or a composition about one of these topics; or use them for further discussion or an oral report.

1. Selling Real Estate
2. A Part-Time Job
3. Caring for Infants/Babies
4. Men and Infant Care
5. Mr./Ms. Forgetful
6. A Bad Habit
7. A Beauty Salon/A Beautician
8. Why I Favor Tipping
9. Why I'm Against Tipping
10. Giving Children Household Chores
11. On the Phone Too Much
12. The Sun Is Bad for Our Skin

IX. Word Families

Complete the sentences with the following words. If necessary, add an ending to the word so it forms a correct sentence. (adj. = adjective and adv. = adverb)

1. **spare** (adj. or verb)   **sparing** (adj.)   **sparingly** (adv.)

   A. We have to be _____ in our use of water. It hasn't rained in weeks.

   B. Regina spends her money _____ . She's saving to buy a house.

   C. Hakim had a flat on his way to school. Fortunately, he had a

   _____ tire in the trunk of his car.

2. **leak** (noun or verb)   **leaky** (adj.)   **leakage** (noun)

   A. The plumber is fixing the _____ faucet.

   B. There's a _____ in my pen. I'm going to throw it out.

   *C. There's a tiny hole in the water tank; the _____ is slight. It's not an emergency.

*There are two possible answers to C.

93

3. **shade** (noun)   **shady** (adj.)   **shadiness** (noun)

   A. We're looking for a _____ spot for our picnic.

   B. Park in the _____ . If you don't, the car will get very hot.

   *C. The _____ of the forest keeps it cool.

*There are two possible answers to C.

X.

A. Synonyms

*Next to each sentence, write a **synonym** for the underlined word or phrase. If necessary, add an ending to the synonym.*

gossip	chore	develop	seek
gap	avert	peek	negotiate

1. Gail is <u>looking for</u> a business partner. _____

2. There's a big <u>difference</u> between what Luis wants to do and what he can do. _____

3. I looked <u>quickly</u> at my friend's check. _____

4. Putting out the garbage is an easy <u>task</u>. _____

5. The government sent troops to the city to <u>prevent</u> a riot. _____

6. The board of education and the teachers' union are meeting to <u>discuss</u> teachers' salaries and benefits. _____

7. Our company is <u>expanding</u> slowly. _____

8. There's a lot of <u>talk</u> at work about the boss and his new secretary.

   _____

B. Antonyms

Using the words below, complete each sentence with an **antonym** *of the underlined word. If necessary, add an ending to the antonym.*

reject	**shade**	**spare**	**fade**
mind	**expire**	**hike**	**choke**

1. Would you <u>like</u> to go shopping with me? Sure, I don't _____ .
2. Shirley is running for mayor. Her campaign is <u>getting stronger</u> and her

   opponents' hopes are _____ .
3. Some airlines have decided to <u>lower</u> their fares, but others plan to

   _____ them.
4. The <u>sun</u> is strong. I'm going to stay in the _____ .
5. A piece of meat got caught in my throat and I almost _____ ,
   but I'm <u>breathing freely</u> now.
6. Bernie <u>accepted</u> my offer, but Stan _____ it.
7. Our lease <u>starts</u> tomorrow and _____ in a year.
8. In World War II, U.S. warplanes bombed and <u>destroyed</u> many places in

   Italy, but they _____ the historic treasures of Rome.

XI. Building Words with -age

The suffix **-age** is added to nouns and verbs and forms a noun. The meaning of **-age** varies widely. It means (a) **the state or condition of being**, for example, **marriage** means **the state of being married:** (b) **the number or amount of**, for example, **mileage** means **the number of miles:** (c) **the price of**, for example, **postage** means **the price of mailing (posting) something:** (d) **a place or home for**, for example, **an orphanage is a home for orphans**.

Noun or *Verb*	*Noun*
band	bandage
cover	coverage
leak	leakage

Noun or *Verb*	*Noun*
link	linkage
marry	marriage
mile	mileage
orphan	orphanage
pack	package
pass	passage
percent	percentage
post	postage
short	shortage
store	storage
use	usage
volt	voltage

Complete the sentences with these words.

bandage	**percentage**	**marriage**	**postage**
voltage	**orphanage**	**storage**	**mileage**

1. I hope you and Sonia have a happy _____ .

2. Did you check the _____ before we started the trip?

3. The doctor put a _____ on my arm.

4. Marcy was raised in an _____ . Her parents died when she was a baby.

5. How much did the _____ stamps cost?

6. Those are high _____ wires. Stay away from them!

7. We want a house with three bedrooms and a lot of _____ .

8. A large _____ of married couples own their own homes.

96

Unit Four
A Family and Its Careers

Ten

A Police Detective

Preview Questions

Discuss or think about these questions before reading the story.

1. What do police detectives do? Do they have a tough job? Is their job interesting? Why or why not?

2. Would you feel proud if a member of your family were a police officer?

3. Would you worry a lot if your husband or wife, or your son or daughter, were a police officer? Explain your answer.

4. Would you be happier if he or she had another type of job?

A Police Detective

Jerry has been a police officer in Philadelphia for twenty years, and he's one of the police department's top homicide detectives. He investigates murders and is given the toughest cases. His work is very interesting, but it's also extremely dangerous.

Two years ago he almost got killed. He was chasing a murder suspect. He shouted to the man to **halt**, but the suspect turned around and shot him in the chest. Jerry was rushed to the hospital, and the doctors were able to save his life. His **wounds** healed, but he still has a **scar** where the bullet hit. His wife Joan wanted him to retire, but he refused to quit. He has a lot of courage and he loves his job.

Right now Jerry is investigating the murder of Reggie Adams. He was a janitor at one of Philadelphia's public schools. He was a nice guy, but he loved to **bet** on horses and play cards at the casinos in Atlantic City. Unfortunately, he lost a lost of money at the racetrack and the casinos. He wasn't a rich man and he should have stopped betting, but he couldn't control his desire to bet.

Reggie kept thinking his luck would change. He borrowed heavily from the mob[1] and **sank** deeper and deeper into debt. He was unable to pay back what he owed and was warned by the mob that he had to pay or else. He knew he was in big trouble; he **begged** for more time. They gave him forty-eight hours, but he wasn't able to get the money. He was shot on his way home from work. There were no **witnesses**.

Jerry is gathering as much information as he can from Reggie's family and friends. He's almost certain that the mob hired Tom Green to murder Reggie, but he doesn't have enough evidence[2] to arrest him and charge him with the crime. He searched Tom's apartment and found a gun, but it wasn't the murder **weapon**.

Jerry questioned Tom for three hours, but he maintained he was innocent. "You can't pin anything on me,"[3] he said. "I was home watching TV when Reggie was murdered."

Jerry didn't believe a word Tom said, but he knows that without witnesses it'll be difficult to build a case against Tom Green. And Tom will have the best lawyers that money can buy. Jerry is discouraged, but he won't give up. He keeps hunting for the evidence that will prove that Tom was the gunman.

1. A **mob** is *a large group of people, in this case, of criminals.*

2. **Evidence** is *an object or fact that shows something is true or that a certain person did something.*

3. **Pin . . . on** is an idiom. It means *to prove that a person did something wrong.*

I. Comprehension Questions

Answer these questions about the story. *Use your judgment to answer questions with an asterisk. Work in pairs or small groups.* The number in parentheses indicates the paragraph in which you will find the answer.

1. What special work does Jerry do in the police department? (1)
*2. Why do you think he is given the toughest cases?
3. What did the suspect do when Jerry told him to halt? (2)
4. Why did Jerry refuse to quit his job? (2)
*5. Do you think the wives or husbands of police officers ever stop worrying about their spouses?
6. Why didn't Reggie stop betting? (3)
*7. Why do you think he went to the mob for a loan?
8. Why is it going to be difficult to discover who murdered Reggie? (4)
9. Why doesn't Jerry arrest Reggie? (5)
*10. How do you think the police know that the gun Jerry found wasn't the murder weapon?
11. What did Tom say he was doing when Reggie was shot? (6)
*12. Who do you think is paying Tom's lawyers?

II. MINI-DICTIONARY — PART ONE

1. **halt** (hôlt) *verb:* to stop; to pause
   noun: a stop; a pause
   "The parade **halted** to allow the cars to go through the intersection."
   "The construction of the new building came to a **halt***because they didn't have enough money to complete it."

   *Halt is often used in the expression *come to a* **halt**.

2. **wound** (wo͞ond) *noun:* an injury that breaks the skin, especially one from a gun or knife
   verb: to cause a wound
   "Call an ambulance. These **wounds** are serious."
   "Many soldiers were **wounded** in the fighting."

3. **scar** (skär) *noun:* a mark left on the skin when a cut or burn heals
   "I still have a **scar** where I cut my finger five years ago."

4. **bet** (bet) *verb:* to agree to give or receive money from another
   depending on who wins a game, race, etc.
   noun: an agreement to give money to or receive it from
   another depending on who wins a game, race, etc.
   "Adam **bet** ten dollars his team would win the game."
   "I put a two-dollar **bet** on a horserace and I won."
   The past tense of **bet** is **bet**.

III.

Complete the sentences with these words. *If necessary, add an ending to the word so it forms a correct sentence. Use each word twice.*

	wound	**halt**	**bet**	**scar**

1. It's extremely difficult, but the government is trying to _____ the shipment of drugs into the United States.

2. Virginia has a tiny _____ on her nose. You can hardly see it.

3. My friend and I made a small _____ on the football game.

4. You're lucky. Your _____ is slight. You'll be okay in a few days.

5. The operation was successful, but it's going to leave a _____ .

6. Traffic on the highway came to a _____ because of a bad accident.

7. No one was killed, but two men were _____ in the gun battle.

8. We never _____ when we play cards. We just play for fun.

5. **sink** (singk) *verb:* to go down, especially to go below the surface of water or other liquid
"The boat had a big hole and it began to **sink**."
The past tense of **sink** is **sank**.

6. **beg** (beg) *verb:* to ask for as a favor
"The man was **begging** for money. He said he was hungry."

7. **wit·ness** (wit′nis) *noun:* a person who sees something happen
verb: to see something happen
"The **witness** told the court he saw the man take the money."
"Several people **witnessed** the plane crash."

8. **weap·on** (wep′ən) *noun:* anything used to attack or defend, especially a gun, knife, or bomb
"The police searched the man for a **weapon**."

V.

Complete the sentences with these words. *If necessary, add an ending to the word so it forms a correct sentence. Use each word twice.*

witness	sink	weapon	beg

1. The ball is light. It won't _____ .

2. Dave _____ the boss not to fire his brother.

3. I didn't start the fight, but I can't prove it. I don't have any

_____ .

4. The United States and the Soviet Union have powerful nuclear

_____ .

5. Little Tommy is _____ to stay up, but his mother won't let him.

6. I threw the rock in the lake and it _____ .

7. Do the security guards carry _____ ?

8. Neil and Barbara got married before a judge and two _____ .

VI. Preview Questions

Discuss or think about these questions before completing the story.

1. Why do older boys (and sometimes girls) join gangs?

2. Why are gangs so dangerous?

3. Are the gangs mostly in poorer neighborhoods? If so, why?

Complete the story with these words.

witnesses	scar	bet	halt
weapons	wound	sank	begged

Carlos's Gang

Carlos was nineteen years old, and he lived on the Lower East Side of Manhattan in New York City. It's a tough neighborhood with a high rate of unemployment. The unemployed seem to do little but stand on the corner, talk, and _____ on numbers.

Carlos was the leader of a neighborhood gang. The boys in it were from seventeen to nineteen years old. They spent a lot of time in the park along the East River. Many of the members of the gang were on drugs, and the park was called "Needle Park." No other gang was supposed to go into it. But one day another gang went there to challenge Carlos's gang. A fight started quickly. Both sides were armed with knives and baseball bats. Knives were the gang's favorite _____ , but one of the boys had a gun.

Some of the older men in the park knew the boys well, and they

_____ them to _____ their fighting and go home, but they wouldn't listen. The boy with a gun shot Carlos in the shoulder just as the police arrived. When he saw the police, he threw his gun in the river and it _____ . However, the police caught the boy and there were several _____ to the shooting.

The police rushed Carlos to Beth Israel Hospital on First Avenue. The _____ was deep, but the doctors were able to remove the bullet. Carlos will be okay in a couple of weeks, but he will have a _____ on his shoulder for the rest of his life.

VII. *Sharing Information*

Discuss these questions in pairs or small groups.

A. A Police Detective

1. There is a lot of violence and crime in the United States, for example, the murder rate in the United States is far higher than in most other countries. Why do you think there is so much crime and violence in the United States?

2. Do you think the amount of violence in movies and on TV is part of the problem? Why does the media give so much publicity to violent crimes?

3. Despite the assassination of President Kennedy and Martin Luther King and the efforts of police associations, it's been very difficult to pass gun control laws in the United States. Do you favor stricter gun control laws? Why or why not?

4. Do you ever buy a lottery ticket? Do you ever go to a racetrack? To a casino?

5. Do you ever bet on anything? If so, on what?

6. Do you think it's okay to bet if you have the money to lose? In other words, do you feel that betting is usually a harmless pastime, or do you think there is something wrong with it?

7. Some people are addicted to betting. What problems can this cause?

8. What do you think were some arguments in favor of allowing casinos in Atlantic City? What were some arguments against them? Would you have voted for or against casinos in Atlantic City? Why?

B. Carlos's Gang

9. A number of people don't have jobs. Is this because of a lack of education and skills? Or is it because there are not enough jobs for everyone? Or are most of these people lazy?

10. What can parents and a community do to keep gangs from forming?

11. Why do so many people take drugs?

12. What are some bad effects of taking drugs?

13. What can be done to keep people from taking drugs?

14. The federal government and the local police seem unable to halt the flow of drugs into our cities. Why?

VIII. Topics for Writing or Speaking

Write a few lines, a paragraph, or a composition about one of these topics; or use them for further discussion or an oral report.

1. A Detective
2. Gun Control
3. Why There Is So Much Crime in the United States
4. Betting, a Terrible Addiction
5. Most Betting Is Okay
6. Betting Is a Waste of Time and Money
7. A Tough Neighborhood
8. A Dangerous Park
9. Why Gangs Attract the Young
10. A Gang
11. The Bad Effects of Taking Drugs
12. A Drug Addict
13. The Fight Against Drugs

IX. Word Families

Complete the sentences with the following words. If necessary, add an ending to the word so it forms a correct sentence. (adj. = adjective and adv. = adverb)

1. **halt** (verb or noun)   **halting** (adj.)   **haltingly** (adv.)

   A. Jan was reluctant to tell us what happened. That's why his speech

   was _____ .

B. Many countries are trying to _____ the spread of AIDS.

C. Gloria speaks English _____ . She's only been in the United States for eight weeks.

2. **bet** (verb or noun)   **better** or **bettor** (noun)

A. Luke is a big _____ . Fortunately for him, he wins a lot.

B. Professional athletes are not allowed to _____ on their own teams.

3. **to sink**   **sinkable** (adj.)   **unsinkable** (adj.)

A. The raft is made of rubber. They say it's _____ .

B. A torpedo hit the battleship and it _____ .

C. When the Titanic hit an iceberg, they discovered it was

_____ .

4. **to beg**   **beggar** (noun)

A. Kelly taught her dog how to _____ for food.

B. I gave the _____ a quarter and hurried on.

X.   *Building Words with -fy (-ify)*

A number of verbs end with the suffix **-fy (-ify)**. **-Fy** means (a) to **make** or **become**, for example, **solidify** means **to make** or **to become solid; clarify** means **to make clear**: (b) to **cause** or **fill with**, for example, **terrify** means **to fill with terror**.

Many **-fy** verbs come not from English nouns or adjectives but from Latin verbs, for example, **clarify, notify, liquefy, certify, identify, purify**, and **terrify**.

Noun or *Adjective*	*Verb*
beauty	beautify
certain	certify
clear	clarify
false	falsify
glory	glorify

Noun or Adjective	Verb
horror	horrify
identity	indentify
intense	intensify
just	justify
liquid	liquefy
notice	notify
pure	purify
simple	simplify
solid	solidify
terror	terrify

Complete the sentences with these words.

intensifying	simplify	terrified	certify
purify	falsified	solidify	beautify

1. This application form is too complicated. We should _____ it.

2. The best way to _____ this water is to boil it.

3. Dan is running for mayor and he's trying to _____ his support among the middle class.

4. When I saw the man had a gun, I was _____ .

5. The state plans to expand and _____ the park.

6. Debbie is in big trouble. She _____ some records.

7. The real-estate agency is _____ its efforts to sell the building.

8. I asked the bank teller to _____ my check.

Eleven

Becoming a Lawyer

Preview Questions

Discuss or think about these questions before reading the story.

1. Do you think most married women today want to work outside their homes, or would most be happy with being a homemaker and mother?

2. Besides earning money, what are some of the satisfactions of working outside the home?

3. What do you think is the main reason why more married women work today than before? Is it mostly for financial reasons or personal satisfaction?

4. If there is no financial need, do you think most husbands would prefer to have their wives stay home?

Becoming a Lawyer

Joan and Jerry have two children, Nancy and Frank. Nancy graduated from the Wharton School of Finance of the University of Pennsylvania and works in New York City. Frank is younger than Nancy and he goes to Georgetown University in Washington, D.C.

When her children were young, Joan was happy to stay home. However, after her son finished high school and went away to college, she decided to go to law school. There wasn't much to do at home. Besides, she wanted her own career. She was bright and had done well in school. Why shouldn't she go to law school?

When Joan told Jerry she wanted to go to law school, he **frowned** and told her she was too old. Joan got angry at him and replied, "That's nonsense. I'm only forty-five and there are plenty of men and women my age in law schools throughout[1] the country. There must be another reason why you don't want me to go to law school."

Jerry is a police detective, and he admitted that one reason for his opposition was that he doesn't like lawyers, especially the **shrewd** ones who defend suspects he thinks are guilty. Defense lawyers are often able to **convince** juries that the suspects he arrests aren't guilty. So most defense lawyers are his **foes**, not his friends. He also feels that judges and juries are too easy on criminals.

Jerry is very macho,[2] and this was his biggest problem with Joan becoming a lawyer. He was afraid his wife would become too independent and make more money than he did. Or maybe she would expect him to cook and help with the housework.

Joan told him he was being very **selfish**. He should think more about her feelings and needs and less about his. He knew she was right, but he needed more time to change his way of thinking. Gradually his opposition **diminished**, and he finally agreed that it was a good idea for her to become a lawyer. He even began to **boast** to some of his friends that his wife was going to be an attorney.

Joan felt she had something to prove to her husband and his friends. So she studied very hard, and last month she graduated *cum laude*[3] from law school. Receiving a law degree was one of the biggest **thrills** of her life. Of course, Jerry was there to congratulate her and share her joy. He only hopes that she won't become one of those shrewd lawyers who defend the people he arrests.

109

1. **Throughout** means *in every part of* or *all through.*

2. **Macho** is a Spanish word that English has borrowed. It means *being a man and having the qualities associated with manhood.*

3. **Cum laude** is a Latin phrase. It means *with praise.* It is said of graduates with high marks.

I. Comprehension Questions

If the sentence is true, write T. If it's false, write F.

_____ 1. Joan didn't like staying home when her children were young.

_____ 2. She was a smart student.

_____ 3. Jerry encouraged her to go to law school.

_____ 4. Joan thought she was too old to go to law school.

_____ 5. Most defense lawyers are Jerry's enemies.

_____ 6. He thinks judges are too easy on criminals.

_____ 7. He likes the ideas of women's liberation.

_____ 8. Joan thought he was thinking too much about himself.

_____ 9. His opposition to Joan's plan diminished quickly.

_____ 10. She did very well in law school.

II. MINI-DICTIONARY — PART ONE

1. **frown** (froun) *verb:* to make lines on your forehead because you don't understand or are unhappy about something
   noun: lines on the forehead that show one doesn't understand or is unhappy
   "Why are you **frowning**? Is something wrong?"
   "Gina's **frown** showed she didn't agree with what I was saying."

2. **shrewd** (shrōōd) *adjective:* wise, especially in practical and business matters
   "No one can fool Ray. He's too **shrewd**."

3. **con·vince** (kən-vins′) *verb:* to cause someone to believe or do something; to persuade
"The doctor **convinced** me to stop smoking."

4. **foe** (fō) *noun:* an enemy
"In World War II, the United States and Germany were **foes**."

III.

Complete the sentences with these words. *If necessary, add an ending to the word so it forms a correct sentence. Use each word twice.*

convince   frown   foe   shrewd

1. The Indians and European settlers were frequently _____.

2. Jim and Ella had a long talk and she _____ her husband to move to a nicer neighborhood.

3. In 1867, the United States purchased Alaska from Russia. It was a

_____ move.

4. Erica _____ as she read the questions on her final exam. It was very difficult.

5. Abraham Lincoln was an honest man, but he was also a _____ politician.

6. Our army is ready to defend our country against its _____.

7. I knew Ralph didn't like my plan when I saw his _____.

8. You cannot _____ me that Communism is good for the poor.

IV. *MINI-DICTIONARY — PART TWO*

---

5. **self·ish** (sel′fish) *adjective:* concerned too much about self and too little about others
"Jessica only thinks about what she wants and needs. She's **selfish**."

6. **boast** (bōst) *verb:* to speak highly of yourself, or your accomplishments, or your possessions

"Drew **boasts** that he's the smartest student in his class."

7. **di·min·ish** (di-min'ish) *verb:* to make or become less; to decrease

"As we get older, our strength and speed **diminish**."

8. **thrill** (thril) *noun:* a feeling of great excitement; the cause of this feeling

verb: to feel great excitement; to cause one to feel great excitement

"Winning the basketball championship was a big **thrill** for the team and coach."

"Helen was **thrilled** when she discovered she had won a million dollars in the lottery."

V.

Complete the sentences with these words. *If necessary, add an ending to the word so it forms a correct sentence. Use each word twice.*

diminish   **selfish**   **boast**   **thrill**

1. The birth of our baby was the greatest _____ of my life.

2. Children are naturally _____ . They have to be taught to share.

3. Muhammad Ali was a famous boxer and he liked to _____ that he was the greatest.

4. It's still raining, but the wind is _____ .

5. Marty is always helping someone. He's not at all _____ .

6. I thought the President was doing a great job, but now I'm not so sure.

   My confidence in him has _____ .

7. Carol Ann was _____ when she received a letter of acceptance to medical school.

8. Our team played poorly today. They have nothing to _____ about.

Discuss or think about these questions before completing the story.

1. Donald Trump is famous and very rich. What do you know about him?

2. Does having a lot of money make a person happy?

3. What are some things money can't buy?

Complete the story with these words.

frowned	convince	selfish	diminish
shrewd	foes	boast	thrilled

Donald Trump

Donald Trump is rich and knows how to get things done. He owns and runs several hotels and casinos in New York and Atlantic City. He has written a best-selling book about himself. He repaired and reopened an ice skating rink[1] in four months when New York City couldn't do it in seven years.

In 1974, Trump decided to buy the Commodore Hotel near Grand Central Station, but first he had to _____ New York City to give him a tax break and a bank to loan him the money to buy and renovate the aging hotel which at that time was losing a lot of money.

The other Manhattan hotel owners _____ at giving Trump a big tax break and said it would be unfair. They were afraid that their profits would _____ if the renovated hotel were a big success. But the city said it was the only way to keep the Commodore open. Trump got a forty-year tax break and two banks loaned him the money. He was _____ . The renovation of the hotel was very successful.

Trump has a lot of wealthy and powerful friends, but he also has his _____ . Edward Koch, the former Mayor of New York City, was one of them. He thought that Trump was _____ , and criticized him for insisting on having his own way. Trump said that Koch was a poor mayor. Both men have big egos and like to _____ about what they have done, but they have also had their failures.

Koch lost a primary election to David Dinkins who went on to become the Mayor of New York City, and in the spring of 1990 Trump ran into serious financial problems. He had borrowed too much and didn't have enough cash to pay back all his loans. The banks helped him out, but his reputation as a _____ businessman was severely damaged. He seemed to have lost the Midas touch.[2]

1. A **rink** is *an area or building with a surface of ice for ice skating or a wooden floor for roller skating.*
2. King **Midas** was an ancient king, and the legend is that everything he touched turned to gold.

VII. *Sharing Information*

Discuss these questions in pairs or small groups.

A. Becoming a Lawyer

1. If they can, do you think it's better for mothers to stay home and take care of their children when they're very young?

2. Who usually takes care of the children if the mother works? Is it easy to get good child care?

3. Do women in the United States have as many opportunities for good jobs and advancement as men, or is there still discrimination against women in the world of work? Explain your answer.

4. Do you think women get equal pay for equal work?

5. What is the situation with working women in different parts of the world? In the Orient—Japan, Korea, India, China? In Latin America? In the Soviet Union and Cuba? In Western Europe? In the Middle East?

6. Do you think most men feel they should earn more money than their wives? If so, why?

7. Wives who work are more independent of their husbands. Do you think this is good?

8. Do you agree with Jerry that the laws and judges in the United States are too easy on criminals? Do you think criminals are often given jail sentences that are too short?

B. Donald Trump

9. There are many poor people in the world and a few who are very rich. Is this unfair? Why can it be dangerous?

10. What, if anything, would you do about it?

11. Do the rich have a responsibility to share their wealth? What are some of the ways they can do this?

12. Do you favor higher taxes for the rich and middle class to provide more government programs for everyone? If so, what kind of programs?

13. How important is money to you?

VIII. *Topics for Writing or Speaking*

Write a few lines, a paragraph, or a composition about one of these topics; or use them for further discussion or an oral report.

1. New Opportunities for Women
2. Combining Motherhood and a Career

3. Should Mothers Stay Home When Their Children Are Very Young?

4. Machismo
5. Machismo Is Dying/Machismo Is Very Much Alive
6. The Laws in the United States Are Too Easy on Criminals
7. A Rich Person
8. The Unequal Distribution of Wealth
9. How to Lessen Poverty
10. Socialism
11. Communism
12. A Shrewd Businessman/Businesswoman

IX. *Word Families*

Complete the sentences with the following words. If necessary, add an ending to the word so it forms a correct sentence. (adj. = adjective and adv. = adverb)

1. **shrewd** (adj.)   **shrewdly** (adv.)   **shrewdness** (noun)

   A. Blanche handles people and problems _____ . That's why she's such a good manager.

   B. Ned's business has been very successful because of his

      _____ .

   C. The governor isn't too smart, but he does a good job because he

      has _____ advisors.

2. **to convince**   **convincing** (adj.)   **convincingly** (adv.)

   A. Pam's a good speaker. She presented her case _____ .

   B. I _____ Nancy and Bob to see a marriage counselor. They've been having problems lately.

   C. The reasons I gave the boss for deserving a raise weren't very

      _____ .

3. **selfish** (adj.)   **selfishly** (adv.)   **selfishness** (noun)
   unselfish (adj.)   **unselfishly** (adv.)   **unselfishness** (noun)

   A. Jenny never considers the feelings and needs of others. She acts

      _____ .

   B. I admire the _____ of the volunteer firefighters.

C. My son refused to let his friends play with his toys. He was being
_____ .

D. Many people work _____ to collect money for the Red Cross.

E. Kyle's _____ keeps him from cooperating with his neighbors.

F. Eva is always looking for ways to help others. She's _____ .

4. **to boast   boaster** (noun)   **boastful** (adj.)   **boastfully** (adv.)

A. I don't blame Joe for speaking _____ about his daughter. She's bright and pretty.

B. Ron is _____ . He frequently tells people what a good athlete he is.

C. Our high-school band is one of the best in the country. They have a right to _____ a little.

D. Tracy talks a lot about her accomplishments. She's a _____ .

5. **thrill** (noun or verb)   **thriller** (noun)

A. What a _____ it was to ride "Space Mountain" at Disney World!

B. We enjoyed the Hitchcock movie. It was a _____ .

X.   Building Words with -ship

The suffix **-ship** is added to nouns and to the adjective **hard**. **-Ship** means (a) **the condition or quality of**, for example, **citizenship** means **the condition of being a citizen**: (b) **the office or occupation of**, for example, **judgeship** means **the office of judge**: (c) **the art of**, for example, **salesmanship** means **the art of a salesman**.

Noun or *Adjective*	*Noun*
author	authorship
champion	championship
citizen	citizenship
companion	companionship
dictator	dictatorship

117

Noun or Adjective	Noun
friend	friendship
hard	hardship
judge	judgeship
leader	leadership
member	membership
owner	ownership
partner	partnership
relation	relationship
salesman	salesmanship
scholar	scholarship

Complete the sentences with these words.

leadership	**citizenship**	**scholarship**	**relationship**
championship	**membership**	**companionship**	**partnership**

1. Lillian is a very smart girl. She won a full _____ to Yale University.

2. The thirteen American Colonies won the War of Independence under the _____ of George Washington.

3. The three lawyers formed a _____ .

4. Roberto came to the United States four years ago. Next year he's going to apply for _____ .

5. My grandmother is lonely. My grandfather died recently and she misses his _____ .

6. The University of Miami won the national college football _____ .

7. Everyone knows there's a close _____ between exercise and good health.

8. Mary Lou is applying for _____ in our club.

118

Twelve

A Stockbroker

Preview Questions

Discuss or think about these questions before reading the story.

1. Stock is the ownership of a company divided into equal parts called shares. Why do companies sell stock?

2. What is a stockbroker? How does a stockbroker make money?

3. What is a stock market?

A Stockbroker

Nancy graduated from the Wharton School of Finance with straight A's, and now she works on Wall Street in New York City. She's a stockbroker for Merrill Lynch, a large brokerage firm. She buys and sells stocks for her clients. She works long hours, but it's exciting work and she loves it.

Nancy studies the stock market and the research reports put out by Merrill Lynch and makes recommendations to people who want to **invest** in stocks. Although Nancy is young and doesn't have a lot of experience, she's shrewd and usually picks winners for her clients. When she picks a loser, she feels bad, but she knows you can't win them all.[1]

Last week was a **grim** one on Wall Street. The stock market **plunged** over a hundred and fifty points because of **soaring** interest rates. It was one of the worst weeks for the stock market since the crash of October 19, 1987, when the market lost over five hundred points in one day.

Although last week was a bad one on Wall Street, Nancy is optimistic. She is convinced that the market will improve soon. She knows it often reaches a **peak**, declines for a week or so, and then **bounces** right back. This is the **pattern** the market has been following lately. Nancy is telling her clients that it's a good time to buy stocks, or at least to keep the ones they have. The market is lower than it's been for some time, and she thinks it will go up in the near future.

However, she's also warning her clients that a lot depends on interest rates. "I believe that interest rates have **peaked**," she says, "and will soon decline. When this happens, I expect to see a **swift** rise in the stock market."

When interest rates are high, people are more likely to put their money in savings accounts and certificates of deposit (CDs),[2] and stocks aren't so attractive. However, when interest rates are low, many people take their money out of savings accounts and buy stock. Of course, buying stocks is always risky. You can lose a lot of money if your stocks go down, or make a lot if they go up.

Although Nancy is a stockbroker, she keeps fifty percent of her savings in the bank. She invests the rest in stock. She has seen the market **plunge** too often to put all her savings in stock. In the stock market, you never know what will happen tomorrow.

1. **You can't win them all** is an expression. It means *you can't be successful all the time.*

2. A **certificate of deposit (CD)** is *a special savings account with a fixed rate of interest.* It must be left in the bank for a specific length of time, for example, a year.

I. Comprehension Questions

Answer these questions about the story. *Use your judgment to answer questions with an asterisk. Work in pairs or small groups.* The number in parentheses indicates the paragraph in which the answer is found.

1. What is Nancy's job? What company does she work for? (1)
2. What does she study before making recommendations to her clients? (2)
*3. Why does she make money even if a client buys a loser?
4. Why did the stock market plunge last week? (3)
*5. Why did many Wall Street employees lose their jobs after the crash of October 1987?
6. What pattern has the market been following lately? (4)
7. What advice is Nancy giving her clients? (4)
8. What does she think will happen to interest rates? (5)
9. Why does the stock market usually go down when interest rates go up? (6)
10. Why does the market usually go up when interest rates go down? (6)
11. Why does Nancy keep fifty percent of her savings in the bank? (7)
*12. Do you think she tells her clients that she keeps half of her savings in the bank? Why or why not?

II. MINI-DICTIONARY — PART ONE

1. **in·vest** (in-vest′) *verb:* to put money into stock, real estate, or a business to make more money: to put time or energy into something to better it
   "Fernando **invested** all of his money in his new store."

2. **grim** (grim) *adjective:* very serious and unpleasant
   "Ellen cried when she got the **grim** news that her husband was badly injured at work."

3. **plunge** (plunj) *verb:* to move down or forward quickly: to dive
   noun: the act of moving down or forward quickly
   "The temperature **plunged** ten degrees in an hour."
   "The company is worried by a recent **plunge** in profits."

4. soar (sôr) *verb:* to move up quickly

"The rocket **soared** into space."

III.

Complete the sentences with these words. *If necessary, add an ending to the word so it forms a correct sentence. Use each word twice.*

> **soar   grim   plunge   invest**

1. We have a lot more sugar than anyone needs. Prices are _____ .

2. Last night I saw *Killing Fields*, a _____ movie about the spread of the Vietnam War into Cambodia.

3. Kim is rich. She made her money by _____ in real estate.

4. I watched the birds as they _____ over the trees.

5. A _____ judge sentenced the man to life imprisonment for murder.

6. The cost of living is _____ . The government should do something.

7. Dennis is conservative. He only _____ in safe stock like the Bell Telephone Companies.

8. Erin _____ into the ocean and went for a swim.

IV.   *MINI-DICTIONARY — PART TWO*

---

5. **peak** (pēk) *noun:* the highest point of a mountain: the highest level of anything

verb: to reach the highest level

"The mountain climbers reached the **peak** of the mountain."

"Business at the shore **peaks** in July and August."

6. **bounce** (bouns) *verb:* to hit a surface and spring up, back, or forward

noun: the act of bouncing: the ability to bounce

"The ball **bounced** over the fence."

"The basketball needs more air. It doesn't have much **bounce**."

7. **pat·tern** (pat′ərn) *noun:* a way of acting that is repeated regularly, or the way something occurs repeatedly: a design, especially on clothing

"I follow the same **pattern** every morning. I get up, shower, dress, eat breakfast, and drive to work."

8. **swift** (swift) *adjective:* fast, quick

"Doug is a **swift** runner. He has won many races."

V.

Complete the sentences with these words. *If necessary, add an ending to the word so it forms a correct sentence. Use each word twice.*

| bounce | swift | peak | pattern |

1. Traffic on the highway usually _____ at eight A.M. and five P.M.

2. The bullet _____ off the soldier's helmet. He was lucky.

3. The police noticed that the robberies followed a similar _____ .

4. Mel got a _____ reply to his letter complaining to the governor about high taxes.

5. The second baseman caught the ball on one _____ and threw to first for the out.

6. The baby's temperature reached a _____ of a hundred and four degrees and then declined slowly.

7. Joy doesn't like to hurry or to make _____ decisions.

8. I like your dress. The _____ is pretty.

VI. *Preview Questions*

Discuss or think about these questions before completing the story.

1. Do you enjoy flying?

2. Are you afraid to fly? A little? A lot? Not at all?

3. What do you usually do when you fly? Read? Sleep? Watch a movie?

Complete the story with these words.

grim   pattern   plunged   swift
soared   invested   bounce   peak

Afraid to Fly

Ann works for a supermarket chain and she's a very successful executive. She likes everything about her job but flying. Her company has its main office in Chicago, but in the last ten years they have _____ heavily in Texas.

The company opened a supermarket in Dallas two years ago. At first the store did very well. A year ago sales and profits reached their _____ , but they have been declining ever since. The company decided to take _____ action, and they sent Ann to Dallas to look into the situation and make recommendations.

Ann was nervous as she boarded the plane to Dallas. She said a little prayer as the plane _____ into the sky. She was beginning to relax when the flight attendant told the passengers to fasten their seat belts.

The pilot was changing their flight _____ because of a bad storm. The plane climbed higher, but it was impossible to fly above the storm. The plane began to _____ up and down in the heavy winds.

Ann looked _____ . She was never so afraid in her life. She remembered reading the story of a plane that lost power in a storm and _____ to the ground. Everyone on the plane died.

Ann started to read a financial report about the store, but she couldn't think. She tried to read *Time* magazine, but it was impossible. The plane finally flew out of the storm and forty-five minutes later landed safely at Dallas Airport. You can imagine how happy Ann was to get off the plane.

VII. *Sharing Information*

Discuss these questions in pairs or small groups.

A. A Stockbroker

1. The price of a share of stock may go up or down. What makes a stock go up?
2. What makes a stock go down? When does a stock lose all its value?
3. What is the difference between investing in stock and gambling?
4. Are you interested in the stock market? Do you ever read the financial section of the newspaper?
5. Does anyone know for sure which way interest rates will go? Why would it be very valuable for an investor to know? And for someone who is going to buy a house?
6. At present, about how much interest can you earn on a one-year CD? Are the rates the same at all banks?
7. If you don't know the interest rates for CDs and mortgages, how can you find out?
8. If you had an extra 50,000 dollars that you wanted to invest, what would you do? Would you buy stock? Buy CDs and keep the money in the bank? Buy some stock and some CDs? Start your own business?

B. Afraid to Fly

9. Have you flown much? Where have you flown from and to?
10. Flying is relatively safe, for example, it's safer than riding in a car. Why then are so many people afraid of flying?
11. What supermarkets in your area have the best prices? Where does your family buy most of its food?
12. Who does most of the food shopping in your family?

VIII. Topics for Writing or Speaking

Write a few lines, a paragraph, or a composition about one of these topics; or use them for further discussion or an oral report.

1. Stocks/The Stock Market
2. Stockbrokers/A Stockbroker
3. The Crash of October 1987
4. Certificates of Deposit
5. Investing Wisely
6. How I Would Invest Fifty Thousand Dollars
7. Food Shopping/A Supermarket
8. Texas
9. A Trip to Texas
10. My First Airplane Trip
11. An Interesting Plane Trip
12. Why I Don't Like to Fly
13. Flying Is Fun

IX. Word Families

Complete the sentences with the following words. If necessary, add an ending to the word so it forms a correct sentence. (adj. = adjective and adv. = adverb)

1. **to invest**   **investor** (noun)   **investment** (noun)

   A. I don't like risky _____ . I put my money in savings accounts and government bonds.

   B. Our company is _____ in new computers.

   C. Lauren is a shrewd _____ . That's why she's so rich.

2. **grim** (adj.)   **grimly** (adv.)   **grimness** (noun)

   A. The newscaster _____ announced that several people lost their lives in the fire.

   B. The photo showed the _____ of the soldiers before the battle.

   C. The National Institute of Health issued a _____ report on the spread of AIDS.

3. **plunge** (verb or noun)   **plunger** (noun)

   A. The water won't go down the drain. Where's the _____ ?

   B. The lifeguard heard a cry for help and immediately _____ into the pool.

126

4. **peak** (noun or verb)   **peaked** (adj.)

A. Our soccer team will have to be at their _____ to win today's game. The other team is very good.

B. Most roofs are _____ , but some are flat.

5. **bounce** (verb or noun)   **bouncer*** (noun)

A. The _____ threw Stan out of the casino.

B. The baseball hit the wall and _____ back.

*A **bouncer** is a big, strong person who invites and, if necessary, makes disorderly people leave a nightclub or similar place.

6. **swift** (adj.)   **swiftly** (adv.)   **swiftness** (noun)

A. The thief ran _____ out of the bank.

B. Everyone is upset by the _____ rise in the price of food.

C. A cheetah is a large cat with long legs. It's known for its

_____ .

X.

A. Synonyms

*Next to each sentence, write a **synonym** for the underlined word or phrase. If necessary, add an ending to the synonym.*

peak	**shrewd**	**plunge**	**wound**
convince	**pattern**	**bet**	**thrill**

1. The nurse examined Ramon's injuries. _____

2. The salesperson tried to persuade me to buy a new vacuum cleaner.

_____

3. Barry gambles a lot, especially on basketball games. _____

4. The Secretary of State is a very clever person. _____

5. Linda loves the danger and excitement of surfing. _____

6. At the high point of the summer season, all the motels are full.

_____

7. I like the <u>design</u> of your wallpaper. It's beautiful. _____

8. The price of gold is <u>going down</u> fast. _____

B. Antonyms

Using the words below, complete each sentence with an **antonym** *of the underlined word. If necessary, add an ending to the antonym.*

selfish	**halt**	**sink**	**diminish**
foe	**swift**	**grim**	**soar**

1. Ken and I were <u>friends,</u> but we had a big fight and now we're

   _____ .

2. Inez had to go to the hospital for surgery. She tried to be <u>cheerful</u> as she

   left, but she looked _____ .

3. The game <u>started</u> an hour ago, but was _____ by a

   sudden storm.

4. If you put an apple in water, it'll <u>float</u>. If you put a penny in water,

   it'll _____ .

5. I'm jealous. My boat is old and <u>slow</u>. My friend's boat is new and

   _____ .

6. Todd is very <u>generous</u>. He spends a lot of time and money helping others.

   His brother Lou is _____ . He only thinks of himself.

7. The roller coaster _____ into the air and then <u>plunged</u>

   toward the ground.

8. We may have to go out of business. Costs are <u>increasing</u> and sales are

   _____ .

XI.   *Building Words with -hood*

The suffix **-hood** is added to some nouns and forms another noun. **-Hood** means **the condition or time of being**, for example, **boyhood** is **the condition or time of being a boy; motherhood** is **the condition of being a mother.**

Noun	*Noun*
bachelor	bachelorhood
boy	boyhood
brother	brotherhood
child	childhood
father	fatherhood
girl	girlhood
knight	knighthood
maiden	maidenhood
man	manhood
mother	motherhood
neighbor	neighborhood
parent	parenthood
priest	priesthood
sister	sisterhood
state	statehood
woman	womanhood

Complete the sentences with these words.

bachelorhood	**neighborhood**	**priesthood**	**fatherhood**
motherhood	**manhood**	**statehood**	**childhood**

1. Robert has two children and takes the responsibility of _____ seriously.

2. We live in a quiet _____ .

3. Alaska was granted _____ in January 1959 and Hawaii in August of the same year.

4. Martha wants to teach in a nursery school. That's why she's studying early _____ education.

5. The training in the marines tested Greg's courage and _____ .

6. Alan is very religious. He's studying for the _____ .

7. Many women today combine _____ and a career.

8. Brad is happily married, but he misses the freedom of _____ .

Unit Five
Newcomers to the United States

Thirteen

The Commonwealth of Puerto Rico

Preview Questions

Discuss or think about these questions before reading the story.

1. Where is Puerto Rico located? How large an island is it? Does it have a large population?

2. What is its political status? Is it an independent country?

3. Is it a state of the United States?

4. Are Puerto Ricans citizens of the United States?

The Commonwealth of Puerto Rico

Puerto Rico is a pretty tropical island one hundred miles long and thirty-five miles wide. It lies about nine hundred miles southeast of Florida with the Atlantic Ocean to the north and the Caribbean Sea to the south. Over three million people live in Puerto Rico. San Juan is the capital and the largest city with a population of 435,000 people.

Puerto Rico is a commonwealth of the United States. The island elects its own governor and representatives and governs itself, but it is not an independent country, nor is it a state of the United States. It is a free state associated with the United States,[1] and all Puerto Ricans are U.S. citizens. However, those who live on the island can't vote in U.S. presidential elections and don't pay federal income taxes. The people speak Spanish, and their culture is basically Hispanic with some Indian and African influence.

Puerto Rico has **coped** well with the challenge of supporting its large population and has a higher per capita income than any country in Latin America. Manufacturing, agriculture, and tourism are the mainstays[2] of the economy.

In 1948, the island began a drive for industrialization called "Operation Bootstrap."[3] It has been extremely successful and over a thousand new factories have located in Puerto Rico. The factories have been attracted by a plentiful supply of workers and by tax breaks. Factories that move to Puerto Rico don't have to pay taxes for ten years. However, jobs on the island are still quite **scarce**, and the unemployment rate is high.

Juan Ayala is one of the many Puerto Ricans who have been helped by "Operation Bootstrap." He lives with his wife Gloria and their three children in Ponce,[4] a large city in the southwestern part of the island. He works in a factory that moved to Ponce from the United States. Juan doesn't make a lot of money, and when it gets hot in the factory, he **sweats** a lot, but he doesn't complain. He's happy to have a steady job.

Gloria works as a cashier at Sears. She likes her job, but she doesn't find it easy to work and to take care of their three children. Fortunately, Gloria's mother lives with them, and she cares for the children while Gloria is at work. The children love her a lot and she is very **fond** of them.

Ponce is a nice place to live, but the weather can be a problem. The area doesn't get much rain, and the city has had several **droughts**. However, in October 1985 it had the opposite problem. It rained steadily for days and Ponce had a terrible **flood**. Juan and Gloria lived near a river and they had to **flee** for their lives. Some of their neighbors weren't so lucky. Two of them **drowned**, and mud slides killed hundreds of people living on a hillside north of the city.

1. In Spanish, Puerto Rico is officially called *El Estado Libre Asociado de Puerto Rico.* The literal translation of this is "The Associated Free State of Puerto Rico." In 1991 the Puerto Rican people are scheduled to vote for statehood, or independence, or an improved commonwealth status.

2. **Mainstay** means *the main support.*

3. The expression "by one's own bootstraps" means *by one's own efforts.* **Operation Bootstrap** is Puerto Rico's effort to help itself.

4. Ponce is the third largest city of Puerto Rico and has a population of 189,046. The Ponce Museum of Art has an outstanding collection of works by famous European and Puerto Rican artists.

I. Comprehension Questions

If the sentence is true, write T. If it's false, write F.

_____ 1. Puerto Rico lies directly south of Florida.

_____ 2. Over three million people live in Puerto Rico.

_____ 3. The President of the United States appoints the Governor of Puerto Rico.

_____ 4. All Puerto Ricans are U.S. citizens and can vote in presidential elections.

_____ 5. Agriculture still plays an important part in the Puerto Rican economy.

_____ 6. Operation Bootstrap has succeeded in industrializing Puerto Rico.

_____ 7. Unemployment is low in Puerto Rico.

_____ 8. Juan complains a lot about his job.

_____ 9. Ponce usually has dry weather.

_____ 10. Juan and Gloria almost lost their lives in a flood.

II. MINI-DICTIONARY — PART ONE

1. **cope** (cōp) *verb:* to successfully handle a difficult situation
   "Edna is blind, but she **copes** well with the help of a seeing-eye dog."

2. **scarce** (skârs) *adjective:* hard to get because of a small supply
   "Meat was **scarce** during the war."

134

3. **sweat** (swet) *noun:* salty fluid that comes through the skin when the body is very hot
   verb: to produce this fluid
   "I like to exercise and work up a **sweat**."
   "This room is hot. I'm **sweating**."
   The past tense of **sweat** is **sweat** or **sweated**.

4. **fond (of)** (fond) *adjective:* having love for; like very much
   "The students are **fond of** their teacher."

III.

Complete the sentences with these words. *If necessary, add an ending to the word so it forms a correct sentence. Use each word twice.*

sweat	fond of	scarce	cope

1. I am very _____ my cousin.

2. Dale lost his job. I wonder how he's _____ with the situation.

3. Kay wiped the _____ off her forehead.

4. Fresh peaches and strawberries are _____ in the winter.

5. Curtis needs help to _____ with his problems.

6. Mary Lou is _____ chocolate candy.

7. Gold is _____ . That's why it's so valuable.

8. Paul _____ a lot when he plays basketball.

IV.   MINI-DICTIONARY — PART TWO

---

5. **drought** (drout) *noun:* a long period of time with little or no rain
   "We're having a bad **drought**. It hasn't rained in three months."

6. **flood** (flud) *noun:* a lot of water covering a usually dry area: a large and sudden increase

verb: to fill or cover a dry area with a lot of water: to increase greatly and suddenly

"We've had three days of heavy rain. If it doesn't stop soon, we're going to have a **flood.**"

"Pan Am had a **flood** of phone calls after the plane crash."

"The water heater broke and **flooded** our basement."

"Requests for student visas **flooded** the U.S. Embassy."

7. **flee** (flē) *verb:* to move quickly away from; to run away from danger

"The tenants are **fleeing** from the burning building."

The past tense of **flee** is **fled.**

8. **drown** (droun) *verb:* to die by being under water and unable to breathe: to kill by keeping under water

"The boat sank in deep water and many people **drowned.**"

"Bonnie is very upset. Someone **drowned** her cat."

V.

Complete the sentences with these words. *If necessary, add an ending to the word so it forms a correct sentence. Use each word twice.*

flee **drought** **flood** **drown**

1. When we have a _____ , we aren't allowed to wash our cars or water the grass.

2. You can't ice-skate today. The ice is thin and you might fall through and

_____ .

3. The thief grabbed Paula's gold chain and _____ .

4. In the spring, the river often overflows and we have a _____ .

5. The drug dealers are _____ . They saw the police coming.

6. Most of the small streams have dried up because of the _____ .

7. Our game has been canceled. The rain has _____ the playing field.

8. They have two lifeguards at the pool to make sure that no one

_____ .

136

VI. Preview Questions

Discuss or think about these questions before completing the story.

1. What are some advantages of working and living on a farm?

2. What are some disadvantages?

3. What are some advantages of living on or near a river. What are some dangers?

Complete the story with these words.

sweat	scarce	flood	drowned
cope	flee	fond	drought

A Dairy Farm near the Mississippi

The Mississippi River is the largest river in the United States. It begins in the state of Minnesota and empties into the Gulf of Mexico near New Orleans. It is 2,330 miles long.

Don has a dairy farm a half-mile from the mighty Mississippi. He owns six hundred acres of land on which he grows corn. He also has over a hundred cows. The soil is fertile and it's a great place for a farm, but when they get a lot of rain, the farmers begin to worry about a _____ . They've had several over the years. Five years ago the river overflowed and everyone had to _____ . Don and his family got out safely, but ten of their cows _____ .

In the summer of 1988, the farmers faced a very different problem. They didn't get a drop of rain for weeks, and the area suffered its worst _____

137

in fifty years. The river was very low. Hay and corn were _____ ,
and the cows didn't get enough to eat. Farmers in other parts of the country helped
out by sending hay.

Several farmers decided to sell their farms. They couldn't _____
with the bad weather, rising costs, and diminishing profits. But Don never gave
serious thought to selling.

He was too _____ of his farm and lifestyle. He loved the fresh
air, the work on the farm, and walking down to look at the river and watch the boats
go by. He had been a farmer for twenty years and had built up the farm by his hard
work and _____ . He was not about to give up and lose everything
he had struggled for. So he prayed for rain and trusted that things would be better
next year.

VII. *Sharing Information*

Discuss these questions in pairs or small groups.

A. The Commonwealth of Puerto Rico

1. Puerto Rico is a commonwealth associated with the United States. What advantages does this association bring to Puerto Rico? What disadvantages?

2. What advantages does this association bring to the United States? What disadvantages?

3. Many Puerto Ricans want their island to become a state of the United States. What advantages would there be in this? What disadvantages?

4. Do you think the island would lose much of its Hispanic culture if it became a state? Would Spanish continue to be the official language of Puerto Rico?

5. A small but active group of Puerto Ricans favor independence. What advantages would independence bring to Puerto Rico? What disadvantages?

6. Do you think independence would help to preserve and strengthen the Hispanic culture of the island?

7. If you were Puerto Rican, what would you favor? The present status, that is, a commonwealth associated with the United States? Or statehood? Or independence?

B. A Dairy Farm near the Mississippi

8. Name some large rivers in the United States. Name some famous rivers in other countries.

9. Does the area you live in ever suffer from floods? What can be done to prevent floods?

10. Many people who are not farmers live in the country. What are some advantages of country living?

11. What are some advantages of city living?

12. Did you ever live in the country? Did you like it? Would you prefer to live in a city or in the country?

VIII. *Topics for Writing or Speaking*

Write a few lines, a paragraph, or a composition about one of these topics; or use them for further discussion or an oral report.

1. The Political Status of Puerto Rico
2. The Economy of Puerto Rico
3. Operation Bootstrap
4. Working in a Factory
5. A Cashier
6. A Drought
7. A Flood
8. A Farmer
9. A Dairy Farm
10. The Advantages of Living in the Country
11. The Advantages of Living in the City
12. The Mighty Mississippi
13. A River
14. The Pollution of Our Rivers

IX. Word Families

Complete the sentences with the following words. If necessary, add an ending to the word so it forms a correct sentence. (adj. = adjective and adv. = adverb)

1. **scarce** (adj.)   **scarcely** (adv.)   **scarcity** (noun)

    A. I can _____ hear you. Speak louder, please!

    B. Water is very _____ in the Sahara desert.

    C. There is a _____ of doctors in some areas.

2. **sweat** (noun or verb)   **sweaty** (adj.)   **sweater** (noun)

    A. The house is cold. I'm going to put on a _____ .

    B. My tee shirt is _____ from jogging.

    C. I don't like to play tennis in the hot sun. I _____ too much.

3. **fond** (adj.)   **fondly** (adv.)   **fondness** (noun)   **to fondle***

    A. Jane looked _____ at her daughter.

    B. Pat _____ the puppy.

    C. Bruno gets along well with Joyce. His _____ for her is obvious.

    D. Edith wants to be a veterinarian. She's _____ of animals.

*__Fondle__ means *to touch lovingly.*

X. Building Words with -ism

The suffix **-ism** is added to nouns and adjectives and forms a noun. Nouns ending in **-ism** usually refer to **the beliefs and practices of a political or religious group.** For example, **Communism** refers to **the beliefs and practices of the Communist party; Protestantism** refers to **the beliefs and practices of the Protestant religion.**

However, **-ism** can have other meanings. **Terrorism** is **the use of terror, especially for political purposes. Journalism** is **the work of writing and publishing newspapers and magazines.**

Noun or *Adjective*	*Noun*
Buddha	Buddhism
capital	capitalism
Catholic	Catholicism
colonial	colonialism
common	Communism
favorite	favoritism
journal	journalism
liberal	liberalism
Marx	Marxism
material	materialism
national	nationalism
patriot	patriotism
Protestant	Protestantism
social	socialism
terror	terrorism
tour	tourism

Complete the sentences with these words.

favoritism	**colonialism**	**Catholicism**	**tourism**
Communism	**patriotism**	**terrorism**	**journalism**

1. Gandhi fought for the freedom of India and the end of _____ .

2. _____ is very important to the economy of Mexico.

3. Sylvia loves her country and is proud of her _____ .

4. I don't like _____ . People should be given jobs because of ability, not politics.

5. Luke wants to write magazine articles. That's why he's taking a course in _____ .

6. _____ is the principal religion of Poland and Spain.

7. Fidel Castro brought _____ to Cuba.

8. _____ makes it dangerous to travel to some places.

Fourteen

From Ponce to New York

Preview Questions

Discuss or think about these questions before reading the story.

A *nuclear* family consists of a mother and father and their children. An *extended* family treats grandparents, aunts, uncles, and cousins as part of the family.

1. Do you think Puerto Rico and Latin American countries have a nuclear or extended family system?

2. Would most of the families in the United States be considered nuclear or extended?

3. What are some of the advantages of the extended family?

4. What are some of the problems with it?

From Ponce to New York

Juan and Gloria's house was old and was located just sixty feet from where two streams **merge**. That's why it was completely destroyed by the flood. They also lost all but a few possessions; however, their most pressing need was a place to live.

Juan and Gloria come from families that are close, and they spontaneously opened up their homes and hearts to Juan and Gloria. In Puerto Rico the extended family comes to the rescue when disaster strikes. So Juan didn't need the help offered by the Red Cross.

Juan, Gloria, and their children lived with his sister and brother-in-law for a while, but then Juan decided to go to the United States. His brother Pedro lives in New York, and he had offered him a job and said he could live with him. It was an offer Juan couldn't refuse.

Gloria and the children drove Juan to the airport. There were tears in their eyes as they kissed and hugged him and said good-bye. Juan and Gloria had decided not to **split** up the children. They would stay in Puerto Rico with their mother. Juan could never work and take care of them. Besides, the children felt closer to their mother. They needed her.

Although Juan wanted to go to New York, he felt sad and lonely as he boarded the plane. He **sighed** as he buckled his seat belt and took a final look at Puerto Rico. The plane roared into the sky and three hours later landed at Kennedy International Airport in New York City. Juan was lucky to have his brother and a job waiting for him, but he was nervous about living in a country whose language and ways he didn't understand, and whose people didn't understand him very well.

Pedro drove Juan from the airport to his house in Queens.[1] Pedro's wife and children and cousin were waiting to greet him. That night some other relatives and friends came to the house, and they had a big party. It was freezing outside, but everyone gave Juan a warm welcome, and he began to feel that life in New York City wouldn't be so bad after all. The party lasted to three in the morning. Juan was weary but happy when he went to bed.

Pedro was a skilled mechanic, and he owned a gas station and auto repair shop in the East Harlem section of Manhattan.[2] At first the only thing Juan could do was to **pump** gas, but he didn't mind. What bothered him was the weather. New York winters can be harsh, and the year Juan arrived they had a lot of snow and cold weather. The first time Juan saw snow he thought it was wonderful, but he soon got tired of it. He dressed as warmly as he could, but he still **shivered** when he went out on very cold days.

The other major problem was his **lack** of English. He had studied English in school in Puerto Rico, but he had never used it. He knew the names of many things, but he couldn't speak or understand English. He complained that Americans spoke English too fast. He decided to enroll in an English as a Second Language program near his brother's house in Queens.

His teacher looked **stern**, and Juan was afraid that she would make fun of his English, but she was kind and class was fun. His English began to improve, but he didn't have many opportunities to practice it. At work, at home, and in his neighborhood everyone but the children spoke Spanish.

Pedro started to teach Juan how to fix cars. He quickly learned to use the **tools** needed to do routine maintenance and repair work. While pumping gas was no fun, Juan loved to work on cars. Besides there is no money in pumping gas, but there is a lot of it in repairing cars.

1. **Queens** is one of the five boroughs of New York City. The other four are Manhattan, the Bronx, Brooklyn, and Staten Island.

2. The **East Harlem** section of Manhattan has long been the home of Puerto Rican and other Hispanic immigrants. Because of this, it is often called "El Barrio."

I.   Comprehension Questions

Answer these questions about the story. *Use your judgment to answer questions with an asterisk. Work in pairs or small groups.* The number in parentheses indicates the paragraph in which the answer is found.

1. Give two reasons why Juan and Gloria's house was completely destroyed by the flood? (1)

2. Who came to their rescue? (2)

*3. Why do you think Juan couldn't refuse his brother's offer of a job in the United States?

4. Why didn't any of the children go with Juan? (4)

*5. Even if he weren't working, do you think Juan would have wanted the responsibility of raising the children? Explain your answer.

6. How did Juan feel as he boarded the plane? (5)

7. Why was he nervous about living in the United States? (5)

8. What was the difference between the welcome Juan received and the weather outside? (6)

*9. Do you think Juan's welcome was an example of the extended family in action? Explain your answer.

*10. How much English does a person have to know to work at a gas station and pump gas?

11. Why didn't Juan learn much English in Puerto Rico? (8)

12. What was he afraid of when he first went to his English class? (9)

13. Why didn't he have many opportunities to speak English in the United States? (9)

14. Give two reasons why Juan would rather fix cars than pump gas? (10)

II. MINI-DICTIONARY — PART ONE

1. **merge** (mûrj) *verb:* to become one or cause to become one;
    to unite or cause to unite
    "The two airlines are going to **merge**."

2. **split** (split) *verb:* to divide what was one: to divide and share
        noun: a division
    "My brother and I **split** the money. He took half and I took half."
    "A disagreement about the war in Vietnam caused a **split** in the Democratic Party."
        The past tense of **split** is **split**.

3. **sigh** (sī) *verb:* to let out a deep and loud breath because of a
worry, sorrow, or feeling of relief

   noun: the action of sighing

   "The test was difficult. Patricia **sighed** several times during it."

   "I read the bill with a **sigh** and put it back in the envelope."

4. **pump** (pump) *verb:* to move or force a liquid, gas, or air in or out
of something

   noun: a machine or instrument to pump a liquid,
gas, or air

   "We **pumped** the water out of the boat."

   "The man used a **pump** to fill the balloons with air."

III.

Complete the sentences with these words. *If necessary, add an ending to the
word so it becomes a correct sentence. Use each word twice.*

pump	merge	sigh	split

1. As I got on the bus, I looked at my watch and _____ . I was
already twenty minutes late for work.

2. The baby swallowed poison and they had to _____ out her
stomach.

3. The class is too large. We'll have to _____ it.

4. The Missouri River _____ with the Mississippi a little north
of St. Louis.

5. Does the gas station have an air _____ we can use?

6. We have three secretaries. They _____ the work we give
them.

7. It doesn't matter which path we take. They _____ in a
half-mile.

8. When the doctor told Joo Hee her mother was very sick, she

   _____ .

146

5. **stern** (stûrn) *adjective:* severe; strict; very firm

   "The judge was **stern** with the thief. He sent him to jail for ten years."

6. **shi·ver** (shiv′ər) *verb:* to shake because of the cold or because of fear

   "This room is very cold. I'm **shivering**."

7. **lack** (lak) *noun:* the absence of what is needed: an amount less than what is needed.

   verb: to not have: to have less than what is needed

   "A **lack** of money kept us from buying the house."

   "In parts of Africa many people died because they **lacked** food."

8. **tool** (tool) *noun:* an instrument used to make, fix, or do something

   "A hammer and saw are the basic **tools** of a carpenter."

   "Words are the **tools** of a writer."

V.

Complete the sentences with these words. *If necessary, add an ending to the word so it forms a correct sentence. Use each word twice.*

lack	shiver	tool	stern

1. I had a flat tire, but I couldn't change it. There were no _____ in the trunk of the car.

2. The farmers are worried about a _____ of rain.

3. Ron's mother is sweet and gentle, but his father is _____ .

4. Eileen started to _____ as soon as she went in the water. It was freezing.

5. Tyrone is smart enough to go to college, but he _____ the desire.

6. The plumber keeps a box of _____ in the back of his truck.

7. I put on a warm sweater; I was _____ .

8. Emily had a heart attack, and the doctor gave her a _____ warning not to smoke.

VI.   Preview Questions

Discuss or think about these questions before completing the story.

1. Name some good jobs that require skill, but don't require much formal education.

2. Do plumbers, carpenters, electricians, and painters make good money?

3. Why is it important for a country to have people who have the desire and ability to work as plumbers, carpenters, electricians, painters, etc.?

Complete the story with these words.

split	pump	tools	shivering
stern	merge	sighed	lack

A Good Plumber

Richie quit school at sixteen. He had just finished his second year of high school, but he didn't want to go on. His parents were very disappointed and angry. His father warned him that he would soon regret quitting school, but his father's _____ words didn't change his mind. Richie didn't like to study or read books, but he wasn't a bad student and he wasn't lazy. He quit because of a _____ of interest.

Richie loved working with _____ , and he could fix anything. After he left school, he got a job as an assistant to a plumber. In three years he became a licensed plumber and started his own business.

148

Two years later he and his friend Mario decided to _____ their businesses. Mario was in the heating and air conditioning business. They could make more money by working together. They agreed to _____ their expenses and profits.

Mrs. Wallace was their first customer. She had a twenty-five-year-old furnace that stopped working in the middle of the winter. She called Mario and Richie. Mario came at once, but by the time he got there the house was cold, and Mrs. Wallace was _____ . Mario looked at the furnace and said it was too old to fix. He replaced it with a new one.

Mrs. Wallace also told Mario her water heater was fifteen years old and had a small leak. Richie came and checked the heater and said it had to be replaced, or the basement would soon be flooded. Mrs. Wallace _____ as she thought about how much all this would cost, but she told Richie to put in a new water heater. He returned an hour later with a new heater and a _____ to empty the water out of the old one.

VII. *Sharing Information*

Discuss these questions in pairs or small groups.

A. From Ponce to New York

1. Tell us a little about your family. How many brothers and sisters do you have? Where do they live? Where do your parents live?

2. How many aunts and uncles do you have? Where do they live? How many cousins do you have? Where do they live?

3. Do you think your family is nuclear or extended? Explain your answer.

4. Do you like cold weather? Do you like snow? Do you mind driving in snowy weather?

5. Describe the weather in the city or town where you were born and grew up. Does the weather there change much from season to season? Does it ever snow? A lot?

6. Do you think people in the United States speak English fast?

7. What is your first language? Do you think you speak it fast? Do others think so?

8. Did you study English before coming to the United States? For how long? Did you learn much? Did you have the opportunity to practice English?

9. What language do you usually speak at home? With your friends? What opportunities do you have to speak English?

10. Is your English improving? What are you doing to improve it?

11. Why is it important that children learn the first language of their parents as well as English?

B. A Good Plumber

12. Are you handy, that is, are you good at fixing things?

13. What is the problem with owning an old house?

14. When you're getting a big job done in your house, how important is it to get at least two or three estimates? Why are most businesses happy to give free estimates?

VIII. Topics for Writing or Discussion

Write a few lines, a paragraph, or a composition about one of these topics; or use them for further discussion or an oral report.

1. My Family
2. The Extended Family
3. The Country I Am from
4. The Day I Came to the United States
5. Why I Like/Hate Winter
6. Learning English
7. The Importance of Finishing High School
8. A Disagreement with My Son/Daughter
9. A Disagreement with My Parents
10. A Handy Person
11. The Advantages of Being a Plumber/Carpenter/Electrician
12. The Problems of Keeping a House in Good Condition

IX. *Word Families*

Complete the sentences with the following words. If necessary, add an ending to the word so it forms a correct sentence. (adj. = adjective and adv. = adverb)

1. **to merge   merger** (noun)

   A. The companies think their _____ will increase profits.

   B. The First National Bank and River City Bank are going to

   _____ next year.

2. **split** (verb or noun)   **splitting*** (adj.)

   A. Bess is so excited. She won the lottery, but she has to _____ the money with another winner.

   B. I can't go to the concert. I have a _____ headache.

   *Splitting means *severe or intense*. Its most common use is to describe a bad headache.

3. **stern** (adj.)   **sternly** (adv.)   **sternness** (noun)

   A. The coach spoke _____ to the team about their poor play.

   B. As soon as I saw my mother's _____ look, I knew I was in trouble.

   C. The police officer's _____ didn't surprise me. I was going eighty miles an hour.

X. Sound-alikes

Sound-alikes are two words (sometimes more) with the same pro-nunciation, but with different spellings and meanings, for example, **son** and **sun; hear** and **here. Sound-alikes** are also called **homophones. Homo** means **same** and **phone** means **sound.**

Common Sound-alikes

be	bee	
break	brake	
close	clothes	
dear	deer	
eight	ate	
for	four	
here	hear	
hole	whole	
I	eye	
meet	meat	
new	knew	
no	know	
one	won	
see	sea	
son	sun	
their	there	
to	too	two
week	weak	
weigh	way	
who's	whose	
would	wood	
write	right	

Complete sentence A with the words below. Then complete sentences B and C with a **sound-alike.**

ate	**no**	**right**	**for**	**be**
to	**dear**	**one**	**their**	**meet**

1. A. I want you to _____ my cousin.

   B. Americans eat a lot of _____ .

2. A. Andy is going _____ the mall.

B. It's _____ cold for swimming.

C. Sara and Ted have _____ children.

3. A. _____ house is beautiful.

B. I love Canada. I want to live _____ .

4. A. Are these flowers _____ me?

B. You have _____ minutes to finish your test.

5. A. We have _____ time to lose.

B. I _____ what you're thinking.

6. A. There's only _____ customer in the store.

B. We _____ the game five to three.

7. A. Who _____ the cake?

B. The gloves cost _____ dollars.

8. A. It's not easy to _____ a parent.

B. A _____ stung me.

9. A. Zach is a _____ friend.

B. I like to hunt, but the _____ was so pretty I couldn't shoot it.

10. A. Turn _____ at the next light.

B. When are you going to _____ to your mother and father?

wood	who's	break	hear	new
I	weigh	weak	close	hole

1. A. How did you _____ your nose?

B. Put on the emergency _____ . The hill is steep.

2. A. _____ found my wallet.

B. There's something in my _____ .

3. A. The kitchen cabinets are made of _____ .

B. _____ you help me, please?

4. A. Dom can't open the window. He's _____ .

B. I'm going to California for a _____ .

5. A. Can you _____ me?

   B. Come _____ a minute.

6. A. How much do you _____ ?

   B. All right. We'll do it your _____ .

7. A. There's a big _____ in the ground.

   B. Did you read the _____ book?

8. A. _____ at the door?

   B. _____ dog is this?

9. A. Please _____ your books and listen carefully.

   B. The _____ are dirty. I have to wash them.

10. A. Joyce bought a _____ car.

    B. We _____ you would come to the party.

Fifteen

At Home in Two Lands

Preview Questions

Discuss or think about these questions before reading the story.

1. When you first came to the United States, was it difficult to get used to the different customs and ways of this country?

2. What are some of the differences between the culture of the country where you were born and that of the United States?

3. Because people face so many changes so quickly when they move from one culture to another, they often suffer "cultural shock." Do you think you suffered this type of shock? Explain your answer.

4. What do you think has more influence on the way you now think, feel, and act—the culture of the United States or that of the country in which you were raised?

At Home in Two Lands

After a couple of years, Juan felt at home in the United States, as well as in Puerto Rico. Like many newcomers to the United States, he was at home in two lands. He also started to make good money repairing cars, much more than he had ever made in Puerto Rico. But he missed his wife and kids a lot, so he took a week off from work and flew back to Ponce.

Gloria and the kids were so happy to see him, but now Gloria and Juan had to make a painful decision. Should Juan move back to Ponce, or should the family move to New York? Juan and Gloria began to **feud**. She loved Puerto Rico and wanted to stay there. It was a better place to raise children. **According** to some of her friends, children learned all kinds of bad things in the big cities of the United States, especially in New York. "Drugs are such a big problem there," she argued, "and I have no desire to learn English and to freeze every winter." Moving to New York and adjusting to life there would be an **ordeal** for her and the kids.

Juan knew all this. He had experienced the shock of moving to a different culture, but he felt his job and future were in the United States. The kids would have all **sorts** of opportunities there. Gloria could find a job in New York, and her mother could live with them.

Finally Gloria and Juan made a deal. She would go to New York in the spring. They would rent an apartment, and the children and her mother would join them after school closed. Gloria and the children would try living in New York. If it didn't work out, they would all return to Ponce.

Gloria arrived in New York on a pleasant day in the early spring. The sun was shining, the snow was **melting**, and the temperature reached fifty degrees. The next day Juan and Gloria started hunting for an apartment. They looked in *El Diario* and the other Spanish newspapers to find out what apartments were available and how much they cost. They needed three bedrooms, and the prices **ranged** from five hundred to twelve hundred dollars a month.

They started by looking at the cheapest apartment. It was a fifth floor walk-up and it was in bad condition. There were cracks in the ceilings and walls; the kitchen and bedrooms were small and the bathroom was tiny. Gloria couldn't **conceal** her disappointment. The super* said to her in Spanish, "What do you expect for five hundred dollars?" "More than this," she replied.

Juan realized he had made a mistake by starting with the cheapest apartment. The next evening they went to a nicer neighborhood and started looking at more expensive apartments. Two weeks later they found one they liked and could afford. It was in the Bronx near Fordham Road. It had three good-sized bedrooms and a modern kitchen, and it was on the second floor. The building also had an elevator. Juan and Gloria signed a one-year lease and paid the first month's rent and the security fee.

The next day Gloria got a job as a cashier at a Shop-Rite supermarket. It was in a Hispanic neighborhood and her Spanish was an **asset**. Of course, Gloria missed her children and mother, but her work and moving into the apartment kept her busy. She liked her new home. It was nice and living in New York City wasn't as bad as she thought it would be, but she still didn't know if she and her family would stay. What do you think they will do?

*Super** is a shortened form of **superintendent**.

I.   Comprehension Questions

If the sentence is true, write T. If it's false, write F.

_____ 1. Juan likes both Puerto Rico and the United States.

_____ 2. Gloria and Juan quarreled about moving to New York.

_____ 3. Gloria said she wouldn't mind the cold weather in New York.

_____ 4. Juan felt their children would have more opportunities in Puerto Rico than in the United States.

157

_____ 5. Gloria moved to New York in the spring, but the children stayed in Puerto Rico.

_____ 6. The weather was bad the day she arrived in New York.

_____ 7. Juan and Gloria liked the first apartment they were shown.

_____ 8. After seeing that apartment, they began to look at more expensive ones.

_____ 9. The apartment they rented had three small bedrooms.

_____ 10. Gloria's knowledge of Spanish helped her at work.

II. MINI-DICTIONARY — PART ONE

1. **feud** (fyo͞od) *verb:* to quarrel, especially to quarrel continually
   noun: a quarrel, especially one that is continual
   "Mike and Frank like politics. Mike is a conservative and Frank is a liberal, and they are always **feuding**."
   "My brother and I were talking about baseball and we got into a big **feud**."

2. **ac·cord·ing to** (ə·kôr′ding to͞o) *preposition:* as stated by: depending on
   "**According to** the weather report, it's going to rain tomorrow."
   "The children were put into groups **according to** their age."

3. **or·deal** (ôr′dēl or ôr·dēl′) *noun:* a very painful or difficult experience
   "Studying for the final exams was an **ordeal**. I'm glad they're over."

4. **sort** (of) (sôrt) *noun:* kind; type
   "There are all **sorts** of people in the world."

III.

Complete the sentences with these words. *If necessary, add an ending to the word so it forms a correct sentence. Use each word twice.*

ordeal   feud   according to   sort

1. I love my sister, but we're very different and we _____ a lot.

2. The trial lasted for three weeks. It was an _____ .

3. I don't think it's the right _____ of college for you.

4. We owe the gas and electric company ninety dollars _____ this bill.

5. What _____ of person is he?

6. The United States and Canada had a _____ over acid rain. Canada felt the United States wasn't doing enough to control air pollution.

7. We had a bad snowstorm and driving to work was an _____ .

8. Sharon didn't do anything wrong. She acted _____ the law.

IV. *MINI-DICTIONARY — PART TWO*

5. **melt** (melt) *verb:* to change from a solid state to a liquid one: to cause a solid to become a liquid by heating
"Put the ice cream in the freezer before it **melts**."

6. **range** (rānj) *verb:* to vary from a low limit to a high one
noun: the amount of variation possible: variety: the maximum distance something can go
"The players on the team **range** in age from thirteen to eighteen."
"The clothing store has a wide **range** of styles."

7. **con·ceal** (kən·sēl′) *verb:* to hide; to keep from being seen or known
"I'm telling you everything I know. I have nothing to **conceal**."

8. **as·set** (as′et) *noun:* anything of value that is owned and can be sold: any valuable quality or skill
"We have a nice house. It's our main **asset**."
"Pam is very smart. Her intelligence is a big **asset**."

V.

Complete the sentences with these words. *If necessary, add an ending to the word so it forms a correct sentence. Use each word twice.*

range   asset   conceal   melt

1. The man _____ a small amount of cocaine in the bottom of his suitcase.

2. Walter is in financial trouble. He's got a lot of bills and no _____ .

3. The recipe says to _____ the butter first and then add flour and milk.

4. In the winter, our temperatures _____ from zero to fifty degrees Fahrenheit.

5. The fire was so hot that the steel _____ .

6. Jackie didn't have time to go to the bank so she _____ the money in her desk.

7. The university offers a _____ of history courses.

8. Tami's good looks are an _____ .

VI. *Preview Questions*

Discuss or think about these questions before completing the story.

Glen is graduating from college with a major in computer science. He plans to join the marines.

1. Why do you think joining the marines is attractive to Glen?

2. How dangerous is it to be a marine in today's world? Explain your answer.

3. What would you say to your son or daughter or your brother or sister if they wanted to join the marines?

Complete the story with these words.

ordeal	feud	ranging	sorts
melted	according to	asset	conceal

A Marine

Glen was in his last year of college and he was going to graduate in two months.

He had majored in computer science. There were many jobs available in his field with salaries _____ from 25,000 to 45,000 dollars a year for a college graduate with a major in computer science. The fringe benefits were also excellent.

However, Glen decided to join the marines instead. Being a marine was his big dream. His father had been a marine, and he thought Glen's joining the marines was a great idea, but his mother didn't like it at all.

Glen's mother made no effort to _____ her fear and anger. _____ her, it was dangerous and stupid for Glen to enter the marines. He could earn a lot more money working for a computer company.

Glen said he wasn't afraid of the danger and making money wasn't the most important thing in life. She was the stupid one. Fortunately their _____ didn't last long. Glen's mother calmed down, and he apologized for calling her stupid. Her opposition _____ gradually, and in the end she even supported his decision. The marines said they would make good use of Glen's knowledge of computers after he finished basic training.

Glen entered the marines on June 30th and was sent to Parris Island for basic training. He was a good athlete and very strong, and that was an _____ . The new marines were kept on the go from early in the morning to late at night, drilling, marching, and going to class.

The first months in the marines are an _____ for everyone.

You must get up early, obey without question, and go through all _____

of drills. And you march until you're ready to drop. It took Glen several weeks to

adjust to life in the marines.

After he finished his basic training, Glen received an appointment to officer-

training school and a three-day leave. He went home to visit his parents and friends.

He looked like a million dollars and his parents were very proud of him.

VII. *Sharing Information*

Discuss these questions in pairs or small groups.

A. At Home in Two Lands

1. For Juan, what are some of the advantages of living in the United States? And some disadvantages?
2. And for you, what are some of the advantages of living in the United States? And some disadvantages?
3. Why is the United States called a land of opportunity? Do you think it still is?
4. What are some of the problems of raising children in the large cities of the United States? Can you think of any advantages?
5. When parents from other countries bring small children to the United States or have children here, what has more influence on the children—the ways of their parents or the culture of the United States?
6. Why is there often a conflict between these children and their parents?
7. There are many jobs in which it is an asset to be bilingual, to know English and another language. Name some of these jobs.

B. The Marines

8. What things in life are more important than money?
9. Why do you think computer science is a popular major in college?
10. What are some of the advantages of a college education?
11. What role should parents play in their children's choice of a career?

12. Why is the basic training of a marine made so difficult? Do you think such training is necessary, or should it be changed?

13. Why is obedience expected and demanded in the marines and all military organizations?

14. Is obedience also expected and demanded in team sports? And in the business world? Explain your answer.

VIII. *Topics for Writing or Speaking*

Write a few lines, a paragraph, or a composition about one of these topics; or use them for further discussion or an oral report.

1. A Tough Decision
2. Why I Came to the United States
3. Adjusting to Life in the United States
4. Cultural Shock
5. Comparing Two Cities (e.g., Lima and New York)
6. Comparing Two Countries
7. The Advantages of a College Education
8. Choosing a Career
9. Computers
10. More Important Than Money
11. Military Training
12. The U.S. Marine Corps
13. Obedience in the Military/ Sports/the Business World

IX. *Word Families*

Complete the sentences with the following words. If necessary, add an ending to the word so it forms a correct sentence. (adj. = adjective and adv. = adverb)

1. **according to** (preposition)   **accord** (noun)   **accordingly** (adv.)
   in accordance (noun)

   A. After negotiating eight hours, we finally reached an _____ .

   B. Angela acted _____ with company regulations. They can't fire her.

   C. _____ the mayor, the city has improved a lot since he took office.

   D. It was very hot and I dressed _____ . I wore shorts and a tee shirt.

2. **to melt   molten*** (adj.)

   A. Steel is made by combining _____ iron and other metals.

   B. The chocolate candy _____ in my mouth.

*__Molten__ means *melted*, but it is used only of melted rock or metal. __Molten__ used to be the past participle of __melt__.

3. **range** (verb or noun)   **ranger*** (noun)   **rangy** (adj.)

   A. Wayne is tall and _____ , and he's a very good basketball player.

   B. The Air Force wants more long- _____ bombers, but Congress is reluctant to spend the money.

   C. The forest _____ are searching for the lost children.

* A **ranger** is *a person who patrols and protects national forests and parks.*

4. **to conceal   concealment** (noun)

   A. Peggy can't _____ her jealousy when she sees her boyfriend flirting.

   B. The Federal Bureau of Investigation (F.B.I.) discovered the drugs and money despite their careful _____ .

X.

A. Synonyms

Next to each sentence, write a **synonym** *for the underlined word or phrase. If necessary, add an ending to the synonym.*

feud	shiver	flee	sort
cope	range	flood	merge

1. The shirts <u>vary</u> in size from small to extra large. _____

2. What <u>kind</u> of restaurant is it? _____

3. The President and Congress are <u>fighting</u>. _____

4. Duke was caught trying to <u>escape</u> from prison. _____

5. The principal is going to <u>combine</u> the two classes; they're small.

_____

6. Turn up the heat. I'm <u>shaking</u>. _____

7. There's a <u>lot of water</u> on the kitchen floor; a pipe broke. _____

8. A stubborn child can be difficult to <u>deal</u> with. _____

B. Antonyms

Using the words below, complete each sentence with an **antonym** *of the underlined word. If necessary, add an ending to the antonym.*

conceal	scarce	split	lack
fond of	melt	drought	stern

1. Billy is _____ school, but he <u>hates</u> homework.

2. In nice weather taxis are <u>plentiful</u>. When it rains, they're _____ .

3. Last year we had a <u>flood</u>. This summer we're having a _____ .

4. Miriam <u>has</u> the brains and training to do the job, but she _____ experience.

5. In the winter, the lake <u>freezes</u>. In the spring, it _____ .

6. The C.I.A. likes to _____ its activities and they're not happy when the press <u>reveals</u> them.

7. Brent is usually <u>gentle</u>, but when he gets angry, he can be very

_____ .

8. The Civil War _____ our country and it wasn't easy to <u>unite</u> it.

XI. *Sound-alikes*

Sound-alikes are two words (sometimes more) with the same pronunciation, but with different spellings and meanings, for example, **mail** and **male; flower** and **flour. Sound-alikes** are also called **homophones**.

bare	bear
do	due	dew
flee	flea
flower	flour
flu	flew
heal	heel
hire	higher
made	maid
mail	male
pair	pear
pale	pail
peek	peak
piece	peace
plane	plain
road	rode
sale	sail
so	sew
soar	sore
stare	stair
steal	steel
wait	weight
waste	waist
where	wear
which	witch

Complete sentence A with the words below. Then complete sentences B and C with a sound-alike.

soar	**bare**	**mail**	**where**	**peak**
do	**plane**	**heal**	**flower**	**so**

1. A. Can you _____ this package for me?

   B. Mark works in the hospital. He's a _____ nurse.

2. A. Most Olympic swimmers reach their _____ before they're twenty.

   B. I'm going to hide Sheila's birthday presents so she can't _____ at them.

3. A. I burned my finger badly, but it's already started to _____ .

   B. This shoe needs a new _____ .

4. A. You're not allowed in the store with _____ feet.

   B. When a _____ is hungry, it's dangerous.

5. A. Look at that rose! What a pretty _____ !

   B. The recipe calls for a cup of _____ .

6. A. If property taxes continue to _____ , we may have to sell our house.

   B. Joe played baseball yesterday. That's why his arm is _____ .

7. A. The _____ is going to take off soon.

   B. Dorothy likes _____ food.

8. A. _____ does Marvin live?

   B. What did Stella _____ to the wedding?

9. A. Food is getting _____ expensive.

   B. Please _____ this button on my coat.

10. A. _____ you speak Spanish?

    B. The train is _____ in five minutes.

    C. Early in the morning there's _____ on the grass.

flee	which	pair	hire	sale
waste	stare	piece	steal	flu

1. A. Our business is growing. We're going to _____ another secretary.

   B. This is the top floor. We can't go any _____ .

2. A. When Sam found out that the police were looking for him, he decided to _____ .

   B. I have to get some _____ powder for our dog.

3. A. Beth didn't go to work today. She has the _____ .

   B. The birds _____ over our house.

4. A. I need a _____ of warm gloves.

   B. Felix is eating a _____ . He loves fruit.

5. A. Why did you _____ at that woman in the restaurant?

   B. Watch your step! The bottom _____ is slippery.

6. A. We're going to Sears. They're having a big _____ .

   B. It's a perfect day to _____ our boat.

7. A. May I have another _____ of pie?

   B. Betsy and Gerry are moving to the country. They want _____ and quiet.

8. A. _____ bus goes to Philadelphia?

   B. This Halloween my daughter is going to be a _____ .

9. A. The pots are made of stainless _____ .

   B. Don't leave the packages in the car. Someone might _____ them.

10. A. The show was terrible. It was a _____ of time and money.

    B. My _____ is thirty-six inches.

Unit Six
Seniors

Sixteen

A Widow and a Dream

Preview Questions

Discuss or think about these questions before reading the story.

1. Do you smoke? Did you ever smoke? If you quit, why and how did you?

2. Why is it so difficult to stop smoking?

3. Why do people start?

4. Smoking can cause lung cancer? Why is it also bad for your throat and heart?

A Widow and a Dream

Helen Rogers is fifty-two years old, and she's a widow. She lives in a small town about fifteen miles outside of Chicago. Her eighty-six-year-old mother lives with her. Helen is a nurse. She's a very calm person; she rarely gets excited, and she never hurries unless it's necessary. She knows how to take it easy. She's a Type-B personality.

Her husband, Karl, was just the opposite. He had to get things done right away and he was always in a hurry. He rarely relaxed. He was a Type-A personality. Karl died of a heart attack four years ago.

Although recent studies have shown that Type-A personalities don't have more heart attacks than others,[1] Karl smoked a lot and had high blood pressure. He was well aware of the **link** between smoking and cancer, but he was **astonished** when his doctor told him that smoking is more likely to cause heart disease than lung cancer.[2]

Helen was upset when she heard this, and she **pleaded** with her husband to stop smoking. Helen's nagging and the doctor's warning made him stop. He went cold turkey[3] for a week, but he couldn't keep it up.

Then he tried to **curtail** his smoking. He was down to three cigarettes a day, but the nicotine habit proved too strong for him. It wasn't long before he was back to smoking two packs a day. "I wished I had never started smoking," he said, "but I'm too old to quit. I'll take my chances." Karl had been smoking for forty years. He started when he was sixteen. It made him feel like a man. It was a mistake.

Karl's death **shattered** Helen's dream of moving to southern California. Helen and Karl hated the cold windy winters of Chicago and wanted to live where winters are mild and there is no snow. Karl had planned to retire early and find a part-time job in San Diego. They were **on the verge of** buying a condo there when he died. Helen was angry at herself and Karl. "I should have insisted that he stop," she said, "and he should have listened to the doctor."

Helen wasn't working when Karl died, but there was a serious **shortage** of nurses, and she had no trouble finding a job at a Chicago hospital. She went back to work because she needed the money and because she knew it wasn't good for her to be **idle**. Naturally she missed her husband a lot and felt lonely, but it helped to keep busy. Her friends also helped her cope with her loss. They knew she needed someone to talk to. Her best friend was a widow and she was especially understanding.

---

1. Earlier research had indicated that Type-A personalities were more likely to have heart attacks, but more recent studies have shown that's not true. However, these studies do link a high level of anger and hostility to heart attacks.

2. "Many smokers do not realize that cigarette smoking is *more likely* to cause heart disease than it is to cause lung cancer." (From **The American Medical Association Guide to Heart Care**, page 77.)

3. To **go cold turkey** is an idiom. It means *to stop completely, not gradually.*

I. Comprehension Questions

Answer these questions about the story. *Use your judgment to answer questions with an asterisk. Work in pairs or small groups.* The number in parentheses indicates the paragraph in which the answer is found.

1. What does the first paragraph tell us about Helen's personality? (1)

2. What does the second paragraph tell us about Karl's personality? (2)

*3. Do you think the differences in their personalities caused conflicts between them? Explain your answer.

4. What did the doctor tell Karl that astonished him. (3)

5. What made him give up smoking? (4)

6. Why did he go back to smoking two packs a day? (5)

*7. Do you think he was too old to quit, or was that just an excuse?

8. Why did he start to smoke? (5)

9. Why did Helen and Karl want to move to southern California? (6)

10. Why was it easy for Helen to get a job? (7)

11. Why did she go back to work? (7)

*12. Why wasn't it good for her to be idle?

II. MINI-DICTIONARY — PART ONE

1. **link** (lingk) *noun:* connection; relationship
   verb: to connect; to join
   "There is a close **link** between good nutrition and good health."
   "The Lincoln and Holland Tunnels and the George Washington Bridge **link** Manhattan and New Jersey."

2. **as·ton·ish** (ə·ston′ish) *verb:* to greatly surprise; to amaze
   "Evelyn **astonished** her teacher by getting a hundred on a difficult exam. She's only an average student."

172

3. **plead** (plēd) *verb:* to ask for a favor with much feeling; to beg

"I **pleaded** with the police office not to give me a ticket, but he wouldn't listen."

4. **cur·tail** (kər·tāl′) to reduce; to cut short

"The government has to **curtail** its spending or raise taxes."

III.

Complete the sentences with these words. *If necessary, add an ending to the word so it forms a correct sentence. Use each word twice.*

astonish   curtail   link   plead

1. Don should _____ his drinking.

2. Sara was badly hurt in a train crash and couldn't move. She _____ for help.

3. It _____ everyone when the President announced he wouldn't run for re-election.

4. Is there a _____ between hot weather and the high crime rates of July and August?

5. Terry discovered her son was taking drugs. She _____ with him to enter a program to get help.

6. All the computers in the room are _____ to a central computer.

7. Bo Jackson _____ the crowd by hitting three home runs in one game.

8. We _____ the meeting when we saw how hard it was snowing.

IV. MINI-DICTIONARY — PART TWO

---

5. **shat·ter** (shat′ər) *verb:* to break into many pieces: to destroy

"The explosion **shattered** most of the windows in the building."

6. **on the verge of** (vûrg əv) *noun + preposition:* very close to (happening)

173

"The two countries were **on the verge of** war, but they settled their differences peacefully."

7. **short·age** (shôr′tij) *noun:* the condition of not having enough
   "If it doesn't rain soon, we're going to gave a water **shortage**."

8. **id·le** (īd′əl) *adjective:* not doing anything; not occupied
   "Larry likes to keep busy. He doesn't like to be **idle**."

V.

Complete the sentences with these words. *If necessary, add an ending to the word so it forms a correct sentence. Use each word twice.*

> idle   shatter   on the verge of   shortage

1. The warm weather _____ our hopes of going skiing.

2. I hope we don't have another gasoline _____ .

3. The factory closed last year and it's still _____ .

4. Sonia was _____ quitting her job when the boss gave her a big raise.

5. There's a _____ of math teachers.

6. My eyeglasses fell on the sidewalk and _____ .

7. The union is unhappy about negotiations with the company. They're

   _____ calling a strike.

8. When young people are _____ , they often get into trouble.

VI.   Preview Questions

Discuss or think about these questions before completing the story.

1. Do you like sweets? Are you fond of chocolate?

2. Do you eat a lot of candy? Cake? Cookies?

3. What problems can eating too many sweets cause?

Complete the story with these words.

link   idle   shortage   astonished
plead   curtail   shattered   on the verge of

Afraid of Diabetes

Sylvia was addicted to all sorts of sweets, and there was never a _____

of candy, cake, or cookies in her home. She was especially fond of chocolate candy

and cake. She had gained a lot of weight, and she didn't like the way she looked. She

was _____ starting a diet.

Before she started her diet, Sylvia went to her doctor for a checkup. She dis-

covered that Sylvia had a high level of sugar in her blood. The doctor explained to her

the _____ between diabetes and being overweight. She warned her

to lose weight and to _____ the amount of sugar she used. The

thought of getting diabetes _____ her peace of mind, and no one

had to _____ with her to start or stay on her diet.

Sylvia _____ her friends by losing twenty pounds in six weeks.

She had no problem sticking to her diet during the day when she was busy and

there was no food around. Her greatest temptation came at night when she was

_____ , and the refrigerator was near.

Before Sylvia started her diet, she used to have several snacks from the time she

finished dinner until she went to bed, but she never ate breakfast. Now she never

misses breakfast and doesn't eat anything after dinner.

VII. Sharing Information

Discuss these questions in pairs or small groups.

A. A Widow and a Dream

1. According to law, a warning is printed on every pack of cigarettes and on all cigarette advertisements. What do these warnings say?

2. What do you think is the best way to stop smoking—to cut down gradually or to go cold turkey?

3. Some people want to protect their right to smoke. Others want to protect their right to breath smoke-free air. Give an example of when these rights come into conflict.

4. Which side do you favor in this controversy? Why?

5. Do you have a calm, take-it-easy, we-can-do-it-later type of personality (Type B)? Or are you an excitable, we-have-to-do-it-now type of person (Type A)?

6. If you're married, what type of personality does your spouse have? If single, what type does your best friend have?

7. Is there still a shortage of nurses? If so, why?

8. There are more widows in the world than widowers. The life expectancy of a woman is about seven years· more than that of a man. Why do women live longer?

B. Afraid of Diabetes

9. What do many diabetics have to take? Why?

10. Is diabetes a dangerous disease? Explain your answer. Is it a common disease?

11. Do you eat much between meals? Do you usually have a snack between dinner and bedtime?

12. What do you usually have for breakfast?

VIII. Topics for Writing or Speaking

Write a few lines, a paragraph, or a composition about one of these topics; or use them for further discussion or an oral report.

1. A Widow
2. A Type-A Personality
3. A Type-B Personality
4. Smoking Is Dangerous to Your Health
5. Why People Smoke
6. How I Stopped Smoking
7. Southern California
8. Fond of Sweets
9. Crazy About Chocolate
10. My Snack Habits
11. Diabetes
12. The Disadvantages of Being Overweight
13. Why I Want to Lose/Gain Weight

IX. Word Families

Complete the sentences with the following words. If necessary, add an ending to the word so it forms a correct sentence. (adj. = adjective and adv. = adverb)

1. **link** (noun or verb)   **linkage** (noun)

   A. All of the major cities in the United States are _____ by modern highways.

   B. The phones and computers are connected, but I think we can improve their _____ .

2. **to astonish**   **astonishment** (noun)   **astonishing** (adj.)
   astonishingly (adv.)

   A. You can imagine Tim's _____ when he came out of the store and discovered his car was gone.

   B. Niagara Falls is _____ beautiful.

   C. The sudden decline of Communism in Eastern Europe _____ me.

   D. Our new computer can store an _____ amount of information.

3. **to plead**   **plea** (noun)   **pleading** (noun)

   *A. The judge listened carefully to the lawyer's _____ for a light sentence for his client.

   B. My friend didn't look well and had pains in her chest and arms. I _____ with her to go to the doctor.

177

*C. When the children realized I wasn't going to let them watch anymore TV, they stopped their _____ and went to bed.

*There are two possible answers to A and C.

4. **to shatter**   **shatterproof*** (adj.)

A. The windshield is made of _____ glass.

B. The temperature reached 100°F and _____ the record high for June.

*The word **shatterproof** is used to describe glass that does not shatter.

5. **shortage** (noun)   **short** (adj.)   **shortly** (adv.)   **to shorten**

A. A sudden shower forced us to _____ our walk.

B. There is a _____ of affordable housing in many parts of the country.

C. The plane will arrive _____ .

D. I went to the bank because I was _____ of cash.

6. **idle** (adj.)   **idly** (adv.)   **idleness** (noun)

A. Josephine sat _____ on the park bench. She had nothing to do.

B. What's the reason for your _____ ? Why aren't you working?

C. When I'm _____ , I think about my problems.

X.   *Look-and-Sound-Alikes*

Look-and-sound-alikes are two or more words that have the same spelling and the same pronunciation, but different meanings and different origins. They are different words that happen to have the same spelling and pronunciation. (n = noun: v = verb: adj. = adjective)

Word	Example	Definition + Part of Speech
1. **box**	"a **box** of candy"	a container (n)
box	"Mike Tyson knows how to **box**."	to fight (v)
2. **can**	"Caroline **can** drive."	to be able to (v)
can	"a **can** of soup"	a metal container (n)
3. **fan**	"a tennis **fan**"	a person with a great interest in a sport (n)
fan	"We need a **fan** to cool the room."	an instrument to move air to cool a person or place (n)
4. **fine**	"I feel **fine**."	very good (adj.)
fine	"I paid a fifty-dollar **fine**."	money paid as a penalty (n)
5. **kind**	"Oscar is a **kind** man."	nice; gentle (adj.)
kind	"What **kind** of food do you like?"	type (n)
6. **mean**	"I know what you **mean**."	to intend to say (v)
mean	"When Chris drinks too much, he gets **mean**."	unkind; not nice at all (adj.)
mean	"The **mean** temperature for July was 78°F."	average; the middle point (adj. or n)
7. **mine**	"That sweater is **mine**."	belonging to me (pronoun)
mine	"a coal **mine**"	a large hole in the ground from which coal or a metal is removed (n)
8. **pitcher**	"a **pitcher** of water"	a container with a handle and a lip, used to hold and pour liquids (n)
pitcher	"Our team has a great **pitcher**."	the baseball player who throws the ball to the hitter (n)

Word	Example	Definition + Part of Speech
9. **race**	"white **race**," "black **race**," "yellow **race**"	*a large division of people with the same origin and physical characteristics (n)*
race	"Who won the **race**?"	*A contest to see who is the fastest (n)*
10. **ring**	"**Ring** the bell."	*to sound a bell; to make the sound of a bell (v)*
ring	"Your wedding **ring** is pretty."	*a band worn on a finger (n)*

Complete the sentences with these words. Use each word twice. *If necessary, add an ending to the word so it forms a correct sentence.*

fan	**box**	**kind**	**can**
mine	**fine**	**pitcher**	**ring**

1. Get up! The alarm clock is _____ .

2. My cousin is a hockey _____ .

3. Rose won't have any trouble getting into a good college. She's a

   _____ student.

4. Chile has many copper _____ .

5. When I need help, I ask Steve. He's _____ .

6. _____ you type?

7. There's a _____ of ice water in the refrigerator.

8. We don't want our son to _____ . It's too dangerous.

9. This room is hot. Do we have a _____ ?

10. They've been playing baseball for two hours. The _____
    are tired.

11. Phil got a ticket for parking in front of a fire hydrant. He has to pay a

    big _____ .

12. The _____ is full of books. It's heavy.
13. That's your pen. Where did I put _____ ?
14. There are many _____ of trees in the forest.
15. Randy's in the kitchen. He's opening a _____ of beans.
16. This _____ is too small. I can't get it on my finger.

Seventeen

Dan's Irish Rose

Preview Questions

Discuss or think about these questions before reading the story.

1. Why is there an increasing number of older people in our population?

2. Older people usually feel that people were friendlier and more honest in the past. What do you think?

3. Many complain that old drivers are often a danger to themselves and others. Do you agree? Explain your answer.

Dan's Irish Rose

Rose Hogan is Helen's mother. She was born in Ireland eighty-six years ago and came to the United States as an infant. Today her hair is gray and her skin is wrinkled, but she was beautiful when she was young. She had light brown hair, pretty blue eyes, and a charming smile. When she was nineteen, she married Dan Hogan and they had five children, four boys and a girl. Dan was an affectionate man, and he liked to call his wife "my Irish Rose." He died ten years ago.

After dinner, Rose likes to watch the seven o'clock news on Channel 4, but she can't stay awake for the whole program. She's okay for about ten minutes, and then she begins to **nod**. By the end of the news she is snoring.

Rose isn't **feeble**, but she can't see or hear well and her memory is poor. Her mind **wanders** a lot, and she lives in the past where, according to her, people were friendlier and more honest, and no one had to lock their doors at night. "Machines get better and better," she says, "but people seem to get worse. There is more stealing, more drugs, and more violence than twenty, thirty, or forty years ago."

Rose is kind and gentle and speaks softly, but she **clings** to her ideas and ways and is very stubborn. For example, Helen has been trying to get her to stop driving, but she won't give up her license. For many **elderly** people, to stop driving is to lose their independence and freedom, and they're naturally reluctant to do so. It took a serious accident to get Rose to agree to give up driving in bad weather and at night.

The accident happened last winter. It began to rain as Rose got into her car to go shopping. The rain quickly turned to sleet, and ice formed on the streets. Driving was very dangerous, but Rose wouldn't turn back. She was driving down a **steep** hill, and she put on the brakes to slow down. She lost control of the car and couldn't **steer**. The car went off the road and crashed into a tree. The car was badly damaged, but fortunately Rose walked away from the accident without a scratch.

In a few years Rose won't be able to take care of herself. She's failing steadily. However, Helen hopes she'll always be able to keep her at home. "I don't want to put my mother in a nursing home," she says. "She would **resent** that very much, and I would feel guilty."

I. Comprehension Questions

If the sentence is true, write T. If it's false, write F.

_____ 1. Rose was pretty and married young.

_____ 2. She has no interest in world events.

_____ 3. Although she's old, her memory is still good.

_____ 4. According to Rose, technology gets better, but people don't.

_____ 5. She frequently changes her mind.

_____ 6. Rose stopped driving at night, but she wouldn't give up her license.

_____ 7. She was driving down an icy hill and smashed into a tree.

_____ 8. She was badly hurt in the accident.

_____ 9. Helen hopes she'll never have to put her mother in a nursing home.

_____ 10. Rose wouldn't mind going into a nursing home.

II. MINI-DICTIONARY — PART ONE

1. **nod** (nod) *verb:* to lower and raise one's head to show agreement or because one is tired
   noun: the act of nodding
   "Ralph came home from work, sat in a soft chair, and started to read the newspaper. Before long, he was **nodding**."
   "Regina asked if I wanted a cup of coffee. I answered with a **nod**."

2. **fee·ble** (fē′bəl) *adjective:* very weak
   "My grandfather can't walk without a cane. He's old and **feeble**."

3. **wan·der** (won′dər) *verb:* to walk or move without a goal or aim
   "We let the dog out every morning, and he **wanders** all over the neighborhood."

184

4. **cling** (kling) *verb:* to hold on to; to hold tightly: to stick to
  "When the little girl is afraid, she **clings** to her mother's skirts."
  The past tense of **cling** is **clung**.

III.

Complete the sentences with these words. *If necessary, add an ending to the word so it forms a correct sentence. Use each word twice.*

> **wander**   **feeble**   **cling**   **nod**

1. The vine is _____ to the tree.

2. Henry didn't have anything to do so he _____ around the city for a while.

3. When I liked what the speaker was saying, I _____ .

4. Doris retired after teaching for fifty years. Her health was poor, and her voice was getting _____ .

5. When I take my son to the mall, I tell him to stay with me and not to _____ off.

6. Gabe only made a _____ attempt to get a job. He was collecting unemployment insurance and was in no hurry to find work.

7. When Irene gave her husband a _____ , he knew she wanted to leave the party.

8. Jerry never changes. He _____ to his habits and tradition.

IV.   *MINI-DICTIONARY — PART TWO*

---

5. **el·der·ly** (el'dər·lē) *adjective:* old or getting old
  "The **elderly** gentleman got on the bus slowly."

6. **steep** (stēp) *adjective:* rising rapidly; having a sharp incline
  "It's extremely difficult to climb that mountain. It's very **steep**."

7. **steer** (stir) *verb:* to direct the course of a vehicle or ship: to guide
   "Regina is **steering** the boat away from the rocks."

8. **re·sent** (ri·zent′) *verb:* to be very angry and offended by someone
   or something
   "What you said about me was unfair and untrue, and I **resent**
   it."

V.

Complete the sentences with these words. *If necessary, add an ending to the word so it forms a correct sentence. Use each word twice.*

resent   **steep**   **elderly**   **steer**

1. The small bus is easier to _____ .

2. The company fired me without an explanation, and I _____
   it.

3. The city has special programs for the _____ .

4. The roof of the church is _____ . It won't be easy to fix.

5. The teacher favors two students, and the others _____ it.

6. Fred is _____ , but he still works very hard.

7. The high-school guidance counselor _____ students to
   colleges she thinks they'll like.

8. The road is flat for a mile or so, but then it gets quite _____ .

VI. *Preview Questions*

Discuss or think about these questions before completing the story.

1. At what age do people usually retire?

2. What are some of the advantages of retirement?

3. How do people support themselves after they retire?

4. In addition to less income, what big problem often comes with retirement?

Complete the story with these words.

resents	wandering	clings	steer
steep	feeble	nods	elderly

Retirement

Sandra Evans is sixty-eight years old. She used to work in a bank, but she retired last year. She's still in good health. "I may be _____ ," she says, "but I feel fine and I'm certainly not _____ ."

When Sandra retired, she had to face two problems. First, she had less money. Her social security check and pension gave her enough to live on, but they didn't equal her salary.

Second, she was restless and unhappy because she didn't have enough to do. One day her daughter asked her if she would take care of her children while she and her husband were at work. Sandra was delighted.

Now she goes to her daughter's house every day to take care of Jessica and Brian. Jessica is two and she's very shy. If a stranger comes to the house, she _____ to her grandmother. Jessica also gets jealous easily and _____ it very much if her grandmother pays too much attention to her brother. Sandra is careful to give her grandchildren equal attention.

Brian is four and he plays in the yard a lot. He will ask Sandra if he can go out. She _____ , and he runs outside. She tells him to be careful going down the stairs. They're _____ , and she's afraid he might fall. The yard has a fence around it, so Sandra doesn't have to worry about her grandson _____ out of the yard.

Brian also likes to ride his new bike on the sidewalk. The bicycle has training wheels so it's easy for him to keep his balance and to _____ .

VII. *Sharing Information*

Discuss these questions in pairs or small groups.

A. Dan's Irish Rose

1. Where is Ireland? What are the political and religious differences between northern and southern Ireland?

2. Why do you think the Irish are still emigrating to the United States in large numbers?

3. What two recent Presidents were Irish Americans?

4. Do you watch the evening news on TV? If so, what channel? Do you sometimes nod and fall asleep when you watch TV at night?

5. Why do older people praise the past so much? Do you agree with Rose that machines get better and better and people seem to get worse? Explain your answer.

6. Is there more stealing, more drugs, and more violence today than in the past? If so, why?

7. Do you think the elderly should be retested at a certain age to make sure they can still drive safely? Explain your answer.

8. Are nursing homes expensive? About how much a year does it cost to live in one?

9. Why are many older people upset when they are placed in a nursing home? Why is it sometimes necessary to put an elderly person in one?

10. Many cultures, for example, oriental cultures, show greater respect for the elderly than we do in the United States. Why?

B. Retirement

11. Grandparents aren't usually as strict with children as parents. Why not?

12. As a child, did you have a lot of contact with your grandparents? Were they important in your life?

13. Are they still alive? If so, where do they live?

14. Do you think shyness is inherited or acquired? In other words, are people born shy, or do they become shy because of the way they are raised?

VIII. *Topics for Writing or Speaking*

Write a few lines, a paragraph, or a composition about one of these topics; or use them for further discussion or an oral report.

1. Ireland
2. An Elderly Person
3. The Elderly and Driving
4. Nursing Homes
5. Machines Get Better, But People Don't
6. The Good Old Days
7. A Car Accident
8. The Advantages of (Early) Retirement
9. The Problems of Retirement
10. My Grandparents
11. The Role of Grandparents
12. Attitudes Toward the Elderly in the United States/Another Country
13. Shyness

IX. *Word Families*

Complete the sentences with the following words. If necessary, add an ending to the word so it forms a correct sentence. (adj. = adjective and adv. = adverb)

1. **feeble** (adj.) **feebly** (adv.) **feebleness** (noun)
   feeble-minded (adj.)

   A. Al's _____ makes it difficult for him to work.

   B. The old gentleman walked _____ to the microphone.

   C. Sally is ninety and can't get out of bed, but she isn't _____ . She understands everything.

   D. Most of the patients at the nursing home are _____ .

2. **to wander**   **wanderer** (noun)   **wanderlust*** (noun)

A. Ernie never lives in one place for long. He's a _____ .

B. Leona loves to travel, but her husband doesn't share her _____ . He prefers to stay home.

C. We _____ around the museum for an hour and then had lunch.

*__Wanderlust__ is *a strong desire to travel or wander.*

3. **elderly** (adj.)   **elder*** (adj. or noun)   **eldest*** (adj. or noun)
elderliness (noun)

A. Leslie and Irving have four children. Their _____ is sixteen.

B. Gene's _____ doesn't keep him from swimming or taking long walks.

C. The subway was crowded so I gave an _____ lady my seat.

D. You should have more respect for your _____ .

*__Elder__ and **eldest**, like **elderly**, are used only to describe people. **Elder** is not used in comparisons with *than*, and *eldest* is used only to describe a family member.

4. **steep** (adj.)   **steeply** (adv.)   **steepness** (noun)

A. The path rises _____ .

B. The _____ of the ladder didn't bother the firefighters.

C. The driveway is _____ .

5. **to resent**   **resentment** (noun)   **resentful** (adj.)
resentfully (adv.)

A. Len looked _____ at the man who had attacked his son.

B. I was there when Jackie insulted you so I understand your

_____ .

C. Marsha's friend didn't invite her to the party, and she's

_____ .

D. How I raise my children is none of your business, and I

_____ your interference.

X. Look-and-Sound-Alikes

Look-and-sound-alikes are two or more words that have the same spelling and the same pronunciation, but different meanings and different origins. They are different words that happen to have the same spelling and pronunciation. (n = noun; v = verb; adj. = adjective; adv. = adverb)

Word	Example	Definition + Part of Speech
1. **last**	"**last** week," "our **last** chance"	*the one before this one: final* (adj.)
last	"The play **lasted** two hours."	*to continue* (v)
2. **light**	"If you're going to read, sit near the window. There's more **light**."	*that which enables us to see* (n)
light	"The suitcase is **light**. It's almost empty."	*having little weight; not heavy* (adj.)
3. **like**	"Harry **likes** to swim."	*to enjoy; to get pleasure from* (v)
like	"Jennifer looks and acts **like** her mother."	*similar to* (preposition)
4. **second**	"I'll be with you in a few **seconds**."	*1/60 of a minute* (n)
second	"This is our **second** trip to Disney World."	*coming next after the first; the ordinal number of two* (adj.)
5. **stern**	"The principal of the school is **stern**."	*strict; severe* (adj.)
stern	"the **stern** of the boat"	*the back part of the boat* (n)
6. **still**	"Does Jean **still** live in Paris?	*before now and at this time too* (adv.)
still	"Don't move! Be **still**!"	*not moving: silent* (adj.)
7. **story**	"What an interesting **story**!"	*an account of an event* (n)
story	"It's a ten-**story** building."	*a floor or level of a building* (n)
8. **tip**	"the **tip** of my finger"	*the top point of something* (n)

Word	Example	Definition + Part of Speech
tip	"Scott gave the taxi-driver a **tip**."	*extra money given to a waiter, beautician, etc.* (n)
9. **well**	"Amy sings **well**." "Are the children **well?**"	*in the right way; in a good way* (adv.): *in good health* (adj.)
well	"We get our water from a **well**."	*a hole dug in the ground to obtain water* (n)
10. **will**	"Alex knows he should stop smoking, but he doesn't have the **will** power."	*firm purpose; human faculty by which we choose* (n): *to choose* (v)
will	"I **will** phone you tonight."	*helping verb used to express future time* (v)

Complete the sentences with these words. Use each word twice. *If necessary, add an ending to the word so it forms a correct sentence.*

still	**last**	**will**	**story**
well	**second**	**tip**	**like**

1. Your diet didn't _____ long.

2. Bonnie _____ country music.

3. Where are we going to get water? The _____ is dry.

4. How many _____ are there in the building where you work?

5. Jessie is fast. He can run a hundred yards in ten _____ .

6. We _____ be some soon.

7. Jamie can't sit _____ . He's hyperactive.

8. Did you give the barber a _____ ?

9. Eileen looks _____ . She just got back from her vacation.

10. Is that a true _____ or did you make it up?

11. It's the _____ day of school. The children are so happy.

12. Is Emily _____ single?

13. This is the _____ parking ticket I've gotten this week.

14. How far is it from here to the _____ of the island?

15. Judy is a good tennis player, and she has the _____ to win. She'll be hard to beat.

16. No wonder Shawn is fat. He eats _____ a horse.

Eighteen

A Marriage Proposal

Preview Questions

Discuss or think about these questions before reading the story.

1. How long do you think couples should know each other before they decide to get married?

2. Do you think marriages later in life are likely to be more stable? If so, why?

3. What are some of the advantages of marrying a doctor? What are some disadvantages?

A Marriage Proposal

Helen enjoys her work as a nurse. She's a kind person and has a warm relationship with her patients and most of the doctors. She especially likes Doctor Sullivan.

He's tall, good looking, and very friendly. Helen admires him because he's the best surgeon in the hospital and is so nice to everyone. He isn't bossy or **greedy** like some doctors who seem more interested in money than their patients.

Doctor Sullivan also liked Helen a lot. After he had gone over a patient's chart with her, he would **linger** for a minute or two to chat. She knew he didn't do this with the other nurses, and she was **flattered** by the special attention he gave her. She enjoyed the closeness they felt.

One day Dr. Sullivan asked her to go out for dinner. She was a little surprised, but she was delighted to go out with him. She didn't know how old the doctor was, but she guessed he was in his early fifties. He was a widower with grown children.

They went to a lovely restaurant and had a very nice dinner. After dinner, they went for a **stroll** in a nearby park. It was a warm evening in June and the moon was full. It was romantic. During a **lull** in their conversation, Dr. Sullivan told Helen he had an important question for her.

"Would you marry me?" he asked. Helen was **stunned** by the question. They were good friends, but she had no idea he was interested in marrying her.

"I like you very much," Helen replied "but this is our first date, and I don't want to **leap** into a marriage I might later regret. I need more time." He said he knew he was being a little **bold,** but he was crazy about her.

The doctor drove her home, invited her to dinner next Saturday and gave her a good night kiss. After that they went dining and dancing every weekend, and they were on the phone a lot. Six weeks later, Helen said yes to Dr. Sullivan's marriage proposal. They got married in the middle of January and had a small reception for their families and a few friends.

The next morning they flew from Chicago to Mexico for their honeymoon. They spent five days in Mexico City and four days in Acapulco. They loved Mexico City with its magnificent art treasures, museums, and beautiful parks. Acapulco was nice too; they liked the beautiful beach and bay, but Mexico City was their favorite.

I. Comprehension Questions

Answer these questions about the story. *Use your judgment to answer questions with an asterisk. Work in pairs or small groups.* The number in parentheses indicates the paragraph in which the answer is found.

1. Why does Helen admire Dr. Sullivan? (2)
2. How did she know Dr. Sullivan liked her? (3)
3. How did she feel about the special attention he showed her? (3)
*4. Do you think the other nurses noticed Dr. Sullivan's interest in her? Explain your answer.
*5. Do you think some of them were jealous? If so, why?
6. What was Helen's reaction to his invitation to dinner? (4)
7. What did Helen and Dr. Sullivan do after dinner? (5)
8. How did she react to his marriage proposal? (6)
*9. Do you think he proposed too soon? Explain your answer.
10. Why didn't Helen say yes to his marriage proposal? (7)
*11. Do you think she was wise to delay her decision? Explain your answer.
12. What did Helen and Dr. Sullivan love about Mexico City? (9)

II. MINI-DICTIONARY — PART ONE

1. **greed·y** (grē-dē) *adjective:* having a very strong desire for more than one needs, especially more money, power, or food
   "All Bert thinks about is how to make more money. He's **greedy**."

2. **lin·ger** (ling′gər) *verb:* to stay longer instead of leaving; to be slow to depart
   "After class, some of the students **lingered** to talk to the teacher."

3. **flat·ter** (flat′ər) *verb:* to praise a person, usually insincerely, to please and win favor
   "When Rudy wants something from his supervisor, he **flatters** her."

4. **stroll** (strōl) *verb:* to walk slowly and for pleasure
            noun: a slow walk for pleasure
            "I like to **stroll** in the woods, especially in the fall."
            "After work, Brenda usually goes for a **stroll** to relax."

III.

Complete the sentences with these words. *If necessary, add an ending to the word so it forms a correct sentence. Use each word twice.*

        flatter   **greedy**   **stroll**   **linger**

1. Don't _____ after the game. Come right home!

2. I think some professional athletes are _____ . They make huge salaries and demand more.

3. Last night Jan and I _____ along the river for an hour.

4. Donna told me that I was the nicest person she had ever met. She was

    _____ me.

5. Ben is wealthy, but he isn't _____ . He gives a lot of money and time to charities.

6. My cold won't go away. It's been _____ for weeks.

7. I _____ Cindy by telling her how much I liked her new dress and hairdo.

8. It's a beautiful day. Let's take a _____ .

IV.   *MINI-DICTIONARY — PART TWO*

---

5. **lull** (lul) *noun:* a period of lessened activity: a pause in activity
            verb: to cause to sleep or be inactive
            "A **lull** in the fighting allowed the soldiers to rest."
            "The soft music **lulled** me to sleep."

6. **stun** (stun) *verb:* to greatly shock
            "Steve's sudden death **stunned** his family and friends."

7. **leap** (lēp) *verb:* to jump, often some distance and suddenly
            noun: a jump, often a long and sudden one
            The past tense of **leap** is **leaped** or **leapt**.

"The dog **leaped** over the fence."

"It took a long **leap** to cross the stream."

8. **bold** (bōld) *adjective:* daring; courageous

"Ralph is shy and quiet, but his brother is **bold** and aggressive."

V.

Complete the sentences with these words. *If necessary, add an ending to the word so it forms a correct sentence. Use each word twice.*

bold	**leap**	**lull**	**stun**

1. The children had a lot of fun _____ into the big pile of leaves.

2. Your idea is _____ , but we like it.

3. I was _____ when the company gave me a big promotion.

4. After a _____ in the storm, it started to rain again.

5. The thief was _____ . He held up a store next to the police station.

6. I know you want to quit school and go to work, but you had better look before you _____ .

7. During a _____ in the interview, the President drank some water.

8. We were _____ when we were told what it would cost to remodel our kitchen.

VI. *Preview Questions*

Discuss or think about these questions before completing the story.

1. What qualities does a good salesperson usually have?

2. Why do some people quit their jobs and go into business for themselves?

3. Why is this difficult to do?

4. Why is it risky?

Complete the story with these words.

stunned	**leap**	**lull**	**flattered**
greedy	**bold**	**linger**	**stroll**

A Business Proposal

Lee and Gene work in a furniture store. They're salesmen and very close friends. When there's a _____ in business and no customers, they chat. When it's time to go home, they often _____ for a few minutes to talk about politics or sports, especially baseball. Lee likes the New York Mets; Gene likes the Los Angeles Dodgers.

Lee loves to talk and he's an excellent salesman. He has a lot of charm and knows how to get people to buy things.

Lee and Gene don't like their boss. He owns the business and is rich. He charges his customers a lot, but he doesn't pay his employees much. He's _____ .

When the weather is nice, Lee and Gene go for a short _____ during their lunch break. One day Lee told Gene he was going to quit his job and open up his own furniture store. It was a _____ move, and Lee asked Gene to quit too and go into business with him.

Gene was _____ by the sudden proposal. He had never thought of quitting. He isn't the type of person who likes to take risks. Lee is.

Lee tried to convince Gene he was the perfect man to work with him. Gene was _____ by Lee's confidence in him, but he said he needed a few days to think about the matter and talk it over with his family.

Gene doesn't want to _____ into a new job and then find himself without work. Lee understands this. He can't guarantee Gene that his business will succeed.

Lee is going to the bank this afternoon to apply for a loan. It'll be two weeks before he hears from the bank, and he can't do anything until then. This will give Gene time to decide.

VII. *Sharing Information*

Discuss these questions in pairs or small groups.

A. A Marriage Proposal

1. Doctors in the United States earn a lot of money. Why do you think their fees are high?
2. How much do doctors who are not specialists charge for an office visit? And specialists? Do you think these fees are too high?
3. Do you think that doctors tend to be bossy? If so, why?
4. Do you have a regular doctor? If so, how would you rate your doctor? Excellent? Very good? Good? Okay? Not so good?
5. Do you think men usually fall in love more quickly than women? Explain your answer.
6. Why do you think Acapulco is a popular spot for honeymoons? Can you name any other popular ones?

B. A Business Proposal

7. Did you ever do sales work? If so, what did you sell? If not, do you think you would like sales work?

8. Do you like to talk about sports? Politics? What are your favorite topics of conversation?

9. Do you have any sports teams you especially like? Which ones? Any players you especially like? Which ones?

10. Walking is excellent exercise. How much do you walk? Do you ever walk just for pleasure and exercise? How often?

11. If you're working, do you like your boss? Is your boss strict? Is he or she fair?

12. What qualities does a good boss usually have?

VIII.   Topics for Writing or Discussion

Write a few lines, a paragraph, or a composition about one of these topics; or use them for further discussion or an oral report.

1. A Great Doctor/Nurse
2. How Nurses Feel About Doctors
3. Doctors in the United States Charge Too Much
4. Doctors Deserve Their High Fees
5. A Marriage Proposal
6. A Honeymoon
7. The Art of Selling
8. A Salesperson
9. The Benefits and Pleasures of Walking
10. Quitting a Job
11. Starting Your Own Business
12. Taking Risks

IX. Word Families

Complete the sentences with the following words. If necessary, add an ending to the word so it forms a correct sentence. (adj. = adjective and adv. = adverb)

1. **greedy** (adj.) **greed** (noun) **greedily** (adv.)

    A. Many crimes are committed because of _____ .

    B. The company is offering Roger a big raise, but he's asking for more. I think he's _____ .

    C. The drug dealers _____ split their profits.

2. **to flatter** **flattery** (noun) **flattering** (adj.) **flatterer** (noun)

    A. I appreciate it when you speak highly of me. It's very _____ .

    B. Carol uses _____ to get what she wants.

    C. Russ says nice things about everyone. He's a _____ .

    D. Mary Ellen _____ her boyfriend by telling him he looks young and handsome.

3. **stroll** (noun or verb) **stroller** (noun)

    A. Delia put her baby in a _____ and went to the store.

    B. In the summer I get up early and go for a _____ before it gets too hot.

4. **lull** (noun or verb) **lullaby*** (noun)

    A. Eddie goes to sleep quickly when I sing his favorite _____ .

    B. To cross the highway, we had to wait for a _____ in traffic.

*A **lullaby** is *a song sung to babies to help them go to sleep.*

5. **to stun** **stunning*** (adj.) **stunningly*** (adv.)

    A. Jacqueline Kennedy was a _____ first lady.

    B. My parents were _____ when they saw my report card. I had failed three subjects.

    C. Everyone at the wedding noticed Lisa. She was _____ dressed.

*Stunning** often means *very beautiful* and **stunningly** *very beautifully.*

6. **bold** (adj.)   **boldly** (adv.)   **boldness** (noun)

   A. General George Patton was known for his bravery and _____ .

   B. Bruce _____ asked his friend for a large loan.

   C. Mikhail Gorbachev, the President of the Soviet Union, is a

       _____ leader and a shrewd politician.

X.

A. Synonyms

Next to each sentence, write a **synonym** *for the underlined word or phrase. If necessary, add an ending to the synonym.*

leap	shatter	stroll	link
stun	curtail	flatter	steer

1. Charley and I went for a <u>walk</u> on the beach. _____

2. The department store hired a security guard to <u>reduce</u> stealing.

   _____

3. My father <u>directed</u> us to the best restaurant in the city. _____

4. Mario <u>jumped</u> into the pool. _____

5. When I discovered that Mike had lied to me, it <u>destroyed</u> my confidence in

   him. _____

6. Julia tried to get a higher grade by <u>praising</u> her teacher. _____

7. They're building a tunnel under the English Channel to <u>connect</u> England

   and France. _____

8. We were <u>shocked</u> when we learned that our son's plane had crashed.

   _____

B. Antonyms

Using the words below, complete each sentence with an **antonym** *of the underlined word. If necessary, add an ending to the antonym.*

elderly	shortage	bold	greedy
idle	linger	resent	feeble

1. The United States usually has a <u>surplus</u> of wheat, and the Soviet Union frequently has a _____ .

2. Howie works in a hardware store. It's very <u>busy</u> so he's almost never _____ .

3. I <u>like</u> friendly advice, but I _____ it when someone tells me what to do.

4. Karen is <u>generous</u>. She's always ready to help a friend in need. Lynn is _____ . Her only concern is to make more money.

5. <u>Young</u> drivers go too fast and _____ ones too slow.

6. Milt is eighty. He used to be very <u>strong</u>, but he's getting _____ now.

7. Most of the people in our office <u>leave</u> work at five o'clock, but I _____ for a short time to talk to my friends.

8. Melissa is <u>timid</u> and fearful. Her cousin Megan is _____ and fearless.

XI. *Shortened Forms*

A number of English words have two forms, a long form and a short one derived from it. The short one is usually informal and in some cases is used more frequently than the long form, for example, **gas, plane, photo,** and **exam** are probably used more frequently than **gasoline, airplane, photograph**, and **examination.**

Long Form	Short Form	Long Form	Short Form
advertisement	ad	photograph	photo
airplane	plane	physical education	phys ed
automobile	auto	professor	prof
bicycle	bike	professional	pro
buttocks	butt	recreation room	rec room
champion	champ	referee	ref
condominium	condo	refrigerator	fridge

Long Form	Short Form	Long Form	Short Form
demonstration	demo	representative	rep
examination	exam	show business	show biz
gasoline	gas	submarine	sub
gymnasium	gym	substitute	sub
handkerchief	hanky(ie)	superintendent	super
high technology	high tech	teenager	teen
hippopotamus	hippo	telephone	phone
information	info	trigonometry	trig
laboratory	lab	typographical error	typo
limousine	limo	umpire	ump
mathematics	math	veterinarian	vet
medical school	med school	veteran	vet
memorandum	memo	vibration	vibe
modern	mod		

Complete the sentences with these shortened words. *If necessary, add an ending to the word so it forms a correct sentence.*

ad	**hippo**	**pro**	**limo**	**bike**
sub	**mod**	**med school**	**champ**	**lab**

1. Vince is a very good football player, but he isn't good enough to be a

   _____ .

2. There are always a lot of _____ in the Sunday newspaper.

3. The chemistry class is in the _____ .

4. Nuclear _____ can stay under water for weeks.

5. Jeff is getting a new _____ for Christmas.

6. Tina wears _____ clothes.

7. We went to the airport in a _____ .

8. Audrey is going to be a doctor. She's starting _____ in
   September.

9. _____ live near rivers, eat plants, and weigh up to five tons.

10. Joe Louis was a great boxer. He was the heavyweight _____
    for many years.

vet	prof	rep	condo	phys ed
memo	sub	fridge	typo	ref

11. The boss sent a _____ to the workers reminding them to be on time.

12. Our history _____ knows a lot, but I don't always agree with her.

13. Gladys sold her house and moved into a _____ .

14. The _____ stopped the fight in the fifth round.

15. There are some oranges in the _____ .

16. Nick's dog was very sick so he took him to the _____ .

17. We play games and do calisthenics in our _____ class.

18. There were so many _____ in the letter that the secretary had to redo it.

19. _____ from the union and the company met to discuss their differences.

20. We had a _____ today. Our regular teacher was absent.

Word List

A

according to 158
  accord 163
  accordingly 163
  in accordance
    163
asset 159
astonish 172
  astonishment
    177
  astonishing 177
  astonishingly 177
avert 80
  aversion 84
  averse 84

B

beg 102
  beggar 106
bet 101
  better or bettor
    106
boast 112
  boaster 117
  boastful 117
  boastfully 117
bold 198
  boldly 203
  boldness 203
bounce 122
  bouncer 127
budget 25
burden 68
  burdensome 73

C

challenge 25
  challenger 29
  challenging 29
charming 4
  charm 9

cheat 56
choke 69
chore 89
cling 185
conceal 159
  concealment 164
convince 111
  convincing 116
  convincingly 116
cope 134
crawl 68
crumb 15
  crumble 19
  crummy 19
curtail 173

D

despite 24
  in spite of 29
develop 69
  developer 73
  development 73
  developmental
    73
dig 89
diminish 112
disappoint 37
  disappointment
    41
  disappointed 41
  disappointing 41
  disappointingly
    41
dread 57
  dreadful 61
  dreadfully 61
drought 135
drown 136

E

elderly 185
  elder 190

eldest 190
  elderliness 190
expand 25
  expanse 29
  expansion 29
  expansive 29
expire 78
  expiration 83
extremely 5
  extreme 10

F

fade 79
fancy 5
feeble 184
  feebly 189
  feebleness 189
  feeble-minded
    189
feud 158
flatter 196
  flattery 202
  flattering 202
  flatterer 202
flaw 46
  flawless 51
  flawlessly 51
flee 136
flood 135
foe 111
fold 4
  folder 9
fond (of) 135
  fondly 140
  fondness 140
  fondle 140
frown 110

G

gap 80
glance 57
gossip 89

grab 70
greedy 196
  greed 202
  greedily 202
grim 121
  grimly 126
  grimness 126

H

halt 100
  halting 105
  haltingly 105
harsh 58
  harshly 61
  harshness 61
heal 37
hide 47
hike 78
hire 25

I

idle 174
  idly 178
  idleness 178
intend 16
  intent 20
  intention 20
  intentional 20
  intentionally 20
  unintentional
    20
  unintentionally
    20
invest 121
  investor 126
  investment 126

J

jealous 46
  jealously 51
  jealousy 51

List of Key Words

Lesson 1

1. fold
2. stare
3. pretend
4. charming
5. reluctant
6. tender
7. fancy
8. extremely

Lesson 2

1. task
2. seldom
3. thorough
4. quarrel
5. toss
6. mess
7. crumb
8. intend

Lesson 3

1. thrive
2. stale
3. steady
4. despite
5. hire
6. expand
7. budget
8. challenge

Lesson 4

1. outstanding
2. twist
3. limp
4. stubborn
5. refuse
6. soak
7. disappoint
8. heal

Lesson 5

1. flaw
2. jealous
3. suspect
4. tease
5. praise
6. hide
7. sneak
8. scold

Lesson 6

1. would rather
2. cheat
3. pressure
4. whisper
5. glance
6. dread
7. harsh
8. regret

Lesson 7

1. crawl
2. mood
3. tickle
4. burden
5. develop
6. choke
7. grab
8. peek

Lesson 8

1. expire
2. seek
3. hike
4. reject
5. fade
6. negotiate
   negotiator
7. avert
8. gap

Lesson 9

1. spare
2. leak
3. chore
4. dig
5. shade
6. gossip
7. mind
8. nag

Lesson 10

1. halt
2. wound
3. scar
4. bet
5. sink
6. beg
7. witness
8. weapon

Lesson 11

1. frown
2. shrewd
3. convince
4. foe
5. selfish
6. boast
7. diminish
8. thrill

Lesson 12

1. invest
2. grim
3. plunge
4. soar
5. peak
6. bounce
7. pattern
8. swift

Lesson 13

1. cope
2. scarce
3. sweat
4. fond (of)
5. drought
6. flood
7. flee
8. drown

Lesson 14

1. merge
2. split
3. sigh
4. pump
5. stern
6. shiver
7. lack
8. tool

Lesson 15

1. feud
2. according to
3. ordeal
4. sort (of)
5. melt
6. range
7. conceal
8. asset

Lesson 16

1. link
2. astonish
3. plead
4. curtail
5. shatter
6. on the verge of
7. shortage
8. idle

Lesson 17

1. nod
2. feeble
3. wander
4. cling
5. elderly
6. steep
7. steer
8. resent

Lesson 18

1. greedy
2. linger
3. flatter
4. stroll
5. lull
6. stun
7. leap
8. bold

REVIEW TEST — UNIT I

*Circle the letter next to the word that **best** completes the sentence.* (Warning! The same word may complete two sentences.)

1. Nancy has many friends. She's a _____ person.

       a. thorough   c. fancy
       b. charming   d. stale

2. I was hurt by Alan's comments, but I _____ that I didn't care.

       a. pretended   c. quarreled
       b. folded   d. intended

3. Cooking is a _____ Fran enjoys.

       a. mess   c. crumb
       b. budget   d. task

4. Larry loves to keep busy. He _____ hard work.

       a. pretends with   c. thrives on
       b. expands with   d. quarrels with

5. Doris was _____ to tell her husband how much the dress cost.

       a. tender   c. steady
       b. fancy   d. reluctant

6. Learning to ski well is a _____ .

       a. quarrel   c. budget
       b. challenge d. mess

7. I _____ to phone my brother, but I forgot.

        a. pretended   c. intended
        b. expanded   d. tossed

8. We're going to play the game _____ the rain.

        a. seldom   c. despite
        b. steady   d. extremely

9. Judy _____ her check and put it in her handbag.

        a. folded   c. challenged
        b. expanded   d. tossed

10. Open the window. The air in this room is _____ .

        a. tender   c. stale
        b. seldom   d. thorough

11. The secretary wants a new typewriter, but there's no money for it in the

_____ .

        a. toss   c. task
        b. budget   d. mess

12. I _____ my keys on the table when I came home.

        a. pretended   c. expanded
        b. folded   d. tossed

13. Mary Ellen is an excellent lawyer. She's very _____ .

        a. stale   c. reluctant
        b. thorough   d. tender

14. Mike is seven feet tall and people often _____ him.

        a. toss   c. challenge
        b. quarrel with   d. stare at

15. We _____ watch TV in the morning; we don't have the time.

      a. seldom   c. steady
      b. thoroughly   d. extremely

16. McDonald's is _____ full- and part-time workers.

      a. folding   c. expanding
      b. challenging   d. hiring

17. The cold weather may kill the tomato plants. They're _____ .

      a. charming   c. tender
      b. fancy   d. steady

18. We had a big party in the gym and now it's a _____ .

      a. challenge   c. budget
      b. mess   d. task

19. Usually Eddie and his friends play nicely, but sometimes they

_____ .

      a. quarrel   c. stare
      b. thrive   d. hire

20. A _____ wind is blowing.

      a. reluctant   c. stale
      b. thorough   d. steady

21. They'll have to _____ our school or build a new one. We need more classrooms.

      a. fold   c. expand
      b. challenge   d. toss

22. Tina should be _____ grateful for your help.

      a. extremely   c. charming
      b. fancy   d. seldom

23. After the picnic, the birds came and ate the _____ left on the ground.

    a. task   c. challenges
    b. crumbs   d. budgets

24. Kurt _____ to write to Edna, but he lost her address.

    a. quarreled   c. folded
    b. intended   d. expanded

25. Craig has a _____ sports car, and he loves to show it off.

    a. fancy   c. thorough
    b. tender   d. steady

REVIEW TEST — UNIT II

Circle the letter next to the word that **best** *completes the sentence.* (Warning! The same word may answer two questions.)

1. Jay will be _____ when you tell him you can't attend his wedding.

        a. cheated   c. twisted
        b. disappointed   d. pressured

2. My cousin has a lovely wife and a great job. Sometimes that makes me a little _____ .

        a. stubborn   c. jealous
        b. outstanding   d. harsh

3. I hope that are no _____ in our new curtains.

        a. flaws   c. suspects
        b. regrets   d. twists

4. No one trusts Walter. He lies and _____ .

        a. limps   c. scolds
        b. refuses   d. cheats

5. Put the dishes in the sink and let them _____ .

        a. heal   c. soak
        b. hide   d. whisper

6. It's not easy to be a coach. There's so much _____ to win.

        a. regret   c. praise
        b. pressure   d. dread

7. The thief is _____ the house.

    a. twisting into   c. praising
    b. whispering to   d. sneaking into

8. Emma is a lawyer and she's _____ . That's why she's so busy.

    a. harsh   c. jealous
    b. outstanding   d. stubborn

9. The firefighters _____ that a cirgarette started the fire.

    a. suspect   c. would rather
    b. dread   d. are whispering

10. I _____ my knee and it still hurts.

    a. cheated   c. twisted
    b. hid   d. scolded

11. Didn't I tell you to stop _____ your sister?

    a. soaking   c. teasing
    b. praising   d. glancing at

12. We want to go swimming, but Matthew _____ play baseball.

    a. is refusing to   c. is hiding to
    b. is cheating to   d. would rather

13. Elsie was in a hurry. So she _____ the newspaper and left for work.

    a. praised   c. whispered to
    b. soaked   d. glanced at

14. Charley _____ the children for playing in the street.

    a. hid   c. healed
    b. twisted   d. scolded

15. Life in prison is _____ .

    a. harsh   c. outstanding
    b. jealous   d. stubborn

16. Kate hurt her foot. That's why she's _____ .

    a. whispering   c. limping
    b. cheating   d. sneaking

17. The operation on Lisa's back was successful, but it'll take a long time to _____ .

    a. hide   c. soak
    b. heal   d. tease

18. The sports writer _____ the team for playing hard although they didn't win.

    a. disappointed   c. praised
    b. suspected   d. pressured

19. Some people like to fly, but I _____ it.

    a. dread   c. glance at
    b. suspect   d. regret

20. The little boy is _____ under the bed.

    a. soaking   c. cheating
    b. hiding   d. limping

21. Jason never admits he's wrong. He's _____ .

    a. outstanding   c. jealous
    b. harsh   d. stubborn

22. Anita thinks she's _____ , but everyone in the room can hear her.

  a. scolding   c. whispering
  b. teasing   d. sneaking

23. I stopped the car and _____ the tire to see if it was flat.

  a. twisted   c. soaked
  b. hid   d. glanced at

24. Eleanor _____ that she didn't buy the house when interest rates were lower.

  a. regrets   c. suspects
  b. would rather   d. dreads

25. Another company is offering me a job that pays a lot more. It's an offer I can't _____ .

  a. pressure   c. cheat
  b. refuse   d. praise

REVIEW TEST — UNIT III

Circle the letter next to the word that **best** *completes the sentence.* (Warning! The same word may answer two questions.)

1. We're never sure how Wanda feels. Her _____ changes quickly.

        a. gap   c. burden
        b. mood   d. crawl

2. Will Jamie _____ if we use his phone?

        a. mind   c. choke
        b. nag   d. gossip

3. This is very good paint. It won't _____ .

        a. tickle   c. expire
        b. leak   d. fade

4. The mechanic _____ under the car so he could fix it.

        a. negotiated   c. gossiped
        b. crawled   d. dug

5. I don't believe that story about Laura. It's only _____ .

        a. shade   c. gossip
        b. a gap   d. a burden

6. Elliot is afraid the publishing company is going to _____ his book.

        a. grab   c. burden
        b. peek at   d. reject

221

7. These coupons aren't any good. They _____ last month.

        a. faded   c. expired
        b. leaked   d. choked

8. Lew was an alcoholic, but he _____ help and has stopped drinking.

        a. averted   c. peeked at
        b. sought   d. grabbed

9. We like the park. It's pretty and has a lot of _____ .

        a. shade   c. leaks
        b. negotiators   d. gaps

10. Stop _____ me! You're making me laugh.

        a. choking   c. tickling
        b. peeking at   d. nagging

11. Almost every year there's a _____ in the cost of living.

        a. crawl   c. hike
        b. leak   d. burden

12. Yoshiko _____ in the classroom, but no one was there.

        a. dug   c. faded
        b. peeked   d. gossiped

13. Your plan seems good, but you'll have to _____ it more.

        a. nag   c. tickle
        b. burden   d. develop

14. Making beds is a _____ I don't like.

        a. chore   c. mood
        b. gap   d. hike

15. I got so angry at Rick I wanted to _____ him.

        a. peek at   c. spare
        b. choke   d. burden

16. Nora is _____ with the car salesperson to get a lower price.

        a. crawling   c. gossiping
        b. negotiating   d. digging

17. There's a _____ in the bottom of the boat.

        a. chore   c. hike
        b. leak   d. reject

18. The thief _____ my wallet and ran down the street.

        a. choked   c. grabbed
        b. peeked at   d. nagged

19. This book will help you _____ your reading skills.

        a. tickle   c. develop
        b. spare   d. nag

20. Claire likes to teach, but she doesn't like the _____ of correcting tests and compositions.

        a. gap   c. mood
        b. crawl   d. burden

21. We don't blame Karen for _____ her son. He's lazy.

        a. nagging   c. seeking
        b. peeking at   d. tickling

22. The United States and Iraq made an unsuccessful attempt to _____ a war over the Iraqi invasion of Kuwait.

        a. choke   c. spare
        b. avert   d. develop

23. The earthquake left a big _____ in the bridge.

        a. chore   c. gap
        b. mood   d. peek

24. The hurricane _____ the beaches and cities along the east coast of the United States by going out to sea.

        a. rejected   c. burdened
        b. grabbed   d. spared

25. Brent is _____ in his garden.

        a. fading   c. nagging
        b. digging   d. expiring

REVIEW TEST — UNIT IV

*Circle the letter next to the word that **best** completes the sentence.* (Warning! The same word may be the answer to two questions.)

1. The lawyer _____ the judge to give his client a second chance.

        a. wounded   c. halted
        b. bet   d. begged

2. In 1960 John Kennedy became the President of the United States after beating Richard Nixon in a close election. Kennedy and Nixon were political

    _____ .

        a. witnesses   c. weapons
        b. foes   d. thrills

3. The tree I chopped down _____ when it hit the ground.

        a. soared   c. bounced
        b. diminished   d. peaked

4. The plastic surgeon carefully removed the growth on my forehead. He didn't want to leave a _____ .

        a. pattern   c. scar
        b. frown   d. witness

5. Our supervisor understands us well. She's a _____ judge of people.

        a. shrewd   c. grim
        b. selfish   d. swift

6. The strike _____ work at the factory.

   a. sank   c. plunged
   b. halted   d. wounded

7. Sergio _____ a lot of time and money in his restaurant, and it's doing well.

   a. diminished   c. bet
   b. plunged   d. invested

8. I play sports because I like the exercise and the _____ of winning.

   a. bounce   c. pattern
   b. thrill   d. peak

9. Peggy _____ her brother to buy a new car.

   a. halted   c. convinced
   b. bet   d. wounded

10. The angry crowd threw stones at the soldiers. Stones were their only

   _____ .

   a. weapons   c. witnesses
   b. scars   d. foes

11. Hugo never worries about other people. He's _____ and has no close friends.

   a. swift   c. shrewd
   b. selfish   d. grim

12. The price of houses is _____ . We're glad we bought one two years ago.

   a. bouncing   c. convincing
   b. thrilling   d. soaring

13. Parents like to _____ their children.

      a. halt   c. boast about
      b. wound   d. bounce

14. The police are looking for a _____ to the crime.

      a. foe   c. halt
      b. witness   d. weapon

15. Stop _____ and tell me what's wrong.

      a. peaking   c. investing
      b. frowning   d. bouncing

16. Ralph lost his job and can't find another. His situation is _____ .

      a. swift   c. selfish
      b. shrewd   d. grim

17. Susan gets upset when her husband _____ and loses a lot of money.

      a. bets   c. begs
      b. soars   d. halts

18. The college is in big trouble. Its enrollment is _____ .

      a. bouncing   c. plunging
      b. convincing   d. boasting

19. The doctor treated the patient's _____ .

      a. witnesses   c. frowns
      b. foes   d. wounds

20. John does a lot in a few hours. He's a _____ worker.

      a. selfish   c. swift
      b. grim   d. thrilling

21. The soldiers _____ to eat and rest.

             a. plunged   c. bet
             b. halted   d. frowned

22. Before the state builds a highway, they study the traffic _____ in the area.

             a. patterns   c. foes
             b. scars   d. witnesses

23. The car went off the bridge and _____ to the bottom of the river.

             a. boasted   c. begged
             b. bounced   d. sank

24. Diane was a professional singer. At the _____ of her career, she was very popular.

             a. pattern   c. peak
             b. thrill   d. halt

25. Bridget is growing up. That's why her interest in dolls is _____ .

             a. bouncing   c. thrilling
             b. convincing   d. diminishing

REVIEW TEST — UNIT V

Circle the letter next to the word that **best** *completes the sentence.* (Warning! the same word may be the answer to two questions.)

1. There's no heat in this car. We're _____ .

   a. sighing   c. shivering
   b. fleeing   d. drowning

2. I got into a (an) _____ with my neighbor when I told him to keep his dog out of our yard.

   a. flood   c. pump
   b. feud   d. ordeal

3. Joan forgot her lunch. I'm going to _____ my sandwich with her.

   a. melt   c. drown
   b. conceal   d. split

4. An ax is a useful _____ , but it can be dangerous if you're not careful.

   a. asset   c. tool
   b. sigh   d. ordeal

5. The price of lettuce has gone way up. It must be _____ .

   a. stern   c. fond
   b. sort of   d. scarce

6. The heart _____ blood to all parts of the body.

   a. pumps   c. conceals
   b. lacks   d. melts

7. Sometimes football practice is fun, but on hot days it's a (an)

   _____ .

   a. sigh   c. drought
   b. ordeal   d. asset

8. The marks on the exam _____ from forty to ninety-five.

   a. split   c. melted
   b. merged   d. ranged

9. A _____ destroyed the old bridge.

   a. pump   c. flood
   b. feud   d. tool

10. Betty is _____ Dennis. They're good friends.

    a. stern with   c. scarce with
    b. coping with   d. fond of

11. When Jake saw the man had a knife, he _____ .

    a. feuded   c. coped
    b. fled   d. melted

12. We need a steady rain to end this _____ .

    a. drought   c. feud
    b. split   d. ordeal

13. The ice is _____ . It's too warm to skate.

    a. sweating   c. melting
    b. merging   d. sighing

14. My children have all _____ of toys.

    a. floods   c. assets
    b. sorts   d. ranges

15. _____ the police officer, I went through a red light.

        a. feuding with   c. according to
        b. coping with   d. sweating with

16. You'll never _____ in our classroom. It has air conditioning.

        a. sigh   c. melt
        b. merge   d. sweat

17. We couldn't stop to visit our friend because of a _____ of time.

        a. lack   c. range
        b. drought   d. split

18. Drive slowly. This road is going to _____ with the highway.

        a. feud   c. melt
        b. flee   d. merge

19. We have a _____ supervisor. He shouts and nags a lot.

        a. fond   c. stern
        b. scarce   d. sweating

20. Regina never swims in deep water. She's afraid of _____ .

        a. sighing   c. shivering
        b. drowning   d. coping

21. The summer camp offers the children a (an) _____ of activities.

        a. range   c. ordeal
        b. sort   d. lack

22. The detective _____ his gun inside his coat.

   a. merged   c. concealed
   b. pumped   d. split

23. Margaret is rich. She has over two million dollars in _____

   a. pumps   c. splits
   b. ordeals   d. assets

24. Matt was in a hurry to get home. He _____ when he saw
the traffic jam ahead.

   a. fled   c. melted
   b. sighed   d. feuded

25. Our company has a new president. I hope she can _____
with the pressure.

   a. merge   c. cope
   b. melt   d. flee

REVIEW TEST — UNIT VI

Circle the letter next to the word that **best** *completes the sentence.* (Warning! The same word may be the answer to more than one question.)

1. Sandy and Dick's divorce _____ everyone.

      a. lulled   c. linked
      b. stunned   d. curtailed

2. Martha said she didn't go to the party because it was raining. That certainly was a _____ excuse.

      a. feeble   c. steep
      b. greedy   d. bold

3. The detectives weren't able to _____ Pete to the crime.

      a. flatter   c. link
      b. steer   d. curtail

4. The government is worried about the _____ of engineers.

      a. lull   c. leap
      b. stroll   d. shortage

5. Robin should go far in politics. She's ambitious, works hard, and is good at _____ people.

      a. stunning   c. curtailing
      b. flattering   d. shattering

6. Our team isn't playing tonight. They're _____ .

      a. greedy   c. idle
      b. bold   d. elderly

7. My sister is always criticizing me and I _____ it.

        a. plead with   c. steer
        b. cling to   d. resent

8. It was snowing lightly, but Ken and Debbie went for a _____ anyway.

        a. leap   c. lull
        b. link   d. stroll

9. Alice _____ with her cousin to slow down. He was driving too fast.

        a. pleaded   c. wandered
        b. lingered   d. nodded

10. Gary loves his new motorcycle. It's light and easy to _____ .

        a. flatter   c. steer
        b. link   d. curtail

11. You're making a good living. Be satisfied with that. Don't get

_____ .

        a. elderly   c. bold
        b. greedy   d. feeble

12. The dress was pretty, but Beth didn't buy it. She didn't like the way it

_____ her.

        a. flattered   c. clung to
        b. pleaded with   d. stunned

13. The police were on the _____ of arresting Kevin when they discovered he was innocent.

        a. link   c. nod
        b. verge   d. leap

14. I was _____ when I heard that my brother had won a million dollars in the lottery.

        a. shattered   c. flattered
        b. curtailed   d. astonished

15. In the United States we glorify youth and don't have enough respect for the _____ .

        a. idle   c. elderly
        b. bold   d. greedy

16. The meeting ended early, but Ray _____ a while to discuss business with a friend.

        a. lingered   c. wandered
        b. pleaded   d. clung

17. The blood bank is asking for donors. There's a _____ of blood.

        a. leap   c. lull
        b. shortage   d. nod

18. The fans _____ their feet and cheered when their team won.

        a. steered with   c. leapt to
        b. wandered on   d. strolled with

19. Vic doesn't hesitate to argue with his boss or anyone else. He's _____ .

        a. feeble   c. bold
        b. idle   d. greedy

20. Eric's nerves were _____ during the Vietnam War, but he's much better now.

        a. curtailed   c. stunned
        b. linked   d. shattered

21. The restaurant is busy from noon to three. There's a _____
    from three to five, and then it's busy again.

            a. shortage   c. leap
            b. nod   d. lull

22. Diego went for a walk in the woods and got lost when he _____
    the path.

            a. clung to   c. linked to
            b. wandered from   d. lingered on

23. Fran is afraid to go on the roller coaster. It's too _____ and
    fast.

            a. bold   c. feeble
            b. greedy   d. steep

24. Emma hasn't been feeling well. She is going to _____ some
    of her activities.

            a. curtail   c. lull
            b. stun   d. shatter

25. I go to school at night, and sometimes I'm so tired that I _____
    in class and even fall asleep.

            a. linger   c. nod
            b. wander   d. plead

Answer Key
Unit One

One
Falling in Love (pages 2–11)

I.	III.	V.	VI.	IX.	X.
1. T	1. charming	1. fancy	1. fancy	1. A. folder	1. impartial
2. T	2. fold	2. tender	2. extremely	B. folded	2. impolite
3. F	3. pretended	3. extremely	3. charming	2. A. pretentious	3. immoral
4. T	4. staring	4. reluctant	4. stared	B. pretends	4. impure
5. F	5. pretending	5. extremely	5. folded	C. pretense	5. impossible
6. F	6. folded	6. reluctant	6. reluctant	3. A. charming	6. immature
7. T	7. charming	7. fancy	7. pretended	B. charmed	7. impatient
8. F	8. staring	8. tender	8. tender	C. charm	8. imbalance
9. T				4. A. reluctance	
10. F				B. reluctantly	
				C. reluctant	
				5. A. tenderly	
				B. tenderness	
				C. tender	
				6. A. extreme	
				B. extremely	
				C. extreme	

Two
Dividing the Housework (pages 12–21)

III.	V.	VI.	IX.	X.
1. seldom	1. intended	1. intends	1. A. thoroughly	1. irresponsible
2. thorough	2. crumbs	2. task	B. thoroughness	2. illiterate
3. quarrel	3. toss	3. mess	C. thorough	3. irregular
4. task	4. mess	4. tosses	2. A. messiness	4. irrelevant
5. thorough	5. toss	5. crumbs	B. mess	5. illegal
6. seldom	6. crumb	6. thorough	C. messy	6. irreplaceable
7. task	7. intend	7. seldom	3. A. crumbs	7. irreversible
8. quarrel	8. mess	8. quarrel	B. crummy	8. illegible
			C. crumbled	
			4. A. unintentionally	
			B. intend	
			C. intentional	
			D. intent	
			E. unintentional	
			F. intentionally	
			G. intentions	

Three
A Thriving Business (pages 22–31)

I.
1. T
2. F
3. F
4. T
5. F
6. F
7. T
8. T
9. T
10. F

III.
1. despite
2. steady
3. thrive
4. stale
5. thriving
6. despite
7. steady
8. stale

V.
1. challenge
2. hire
3. budget
4. expands
5. challenge
6. hired
7. budget
8. expand

VI.
1. steady
2. despite
3. expanding
4. thriving
5. hire
6. challenge
7. stale
8. budget

IX.
1. A. steadily
   B. steadiness
   C. steady
3. A. expansive
   B. expand
   C. expansion
   D. expanse
4. A. challenger
   B. challenged
   C. challenging

X.
1. pretending
2. extremely
3. quarrel
4. thorough
5. thriving
6. intends
7. tossed
8. task

1. steady
2. hiring
3. fancy
4. seldom
5. reluctant
6. stale
7. despite
8. expands

XI.
1. cooperative
2. expensive
3. talkative
4. defective
5. decisive
6. representative
7. active
8. protective

Review Test
(pages 213–216)

1. b	9. a	17. c
2. a	10. c	18. b
3. d	11. b	19. a
4. c	12. d	20. d
5. d	13. b	21. c
6. b	14. d	22. a
7. c	15. a	23. b
8. c	16. d	24. b
		25. a

Unit Two

Four
A Great Basketball Player (pages 34–43)

III.
1. outstanding
2. twist
3. limping
4. stubborn
5. twisted
6. outstanding
7. stubborn
8. limping

V.
1. disappoint
2. soaked
3. refused
4. healed
5. disappointed
6. refused
7. heal
8. soak

VI.
1. oustanding
2. refused
3. stubborn
4. twisted
5. disappointed
6. limping
7. soaked
8. healed

IX.
1. A. stubbornly
   B. stubbornness
   C. stubborn
2. A. refusal
   B. refused
3. A. soak
   B. soaked
4. A. disappointed
   B. disappointingly
   C. disappoint
   D. disappointing
   E. disappointment

X.
1. traditional
2. accidental
3. professional
4. financial
5. arrival
6. denial
7. original
8. additional

Five
Ray's Sweetheart (pages 44–53)

I.	III.	V.	VI.	IX.	X.
1. F	1. suspect	1. praised	1. jealous	1. A. flawlessly	1. responsibility
2. T	suspected	2. hides	2. tease	B. flaws	2. difficulty
3. F	2. jealous	3. sneaks	3. flaw	C. flawless	3. community
4. F	3. flaw	4. scold	4. suspect	2. A. jealously	4. opportunity
5. T	4. tease	5. hide	5. scolds	B. jealousy	5. popularity
6. T	5. jealous	6. praise	6. praises	C. jealous	6. ability
7. T	6. teasing	7. scold	7. sneaks	3. A. suspicious	7. honesty
8. F	7. suspects	8. sneaked	8. hide	B. suspect	8. electricity
9. T	8. flaws	snuck		C. suspiciously	
10. F				D. suspicion	
				4. A. sneaking	
				B. sneakers	
				C. sneaky	
				5. A. scolding	
				B. scolded	

Six
Cheating on a Test (pages 54–64)

III.	V.	VI.	IX.
1. pressure	1. dreads	1. whispered	1. A. pressed
2. whispering	2. regrets	2. glanced	B. pressure
3. would rather	3. glanced	3. would rather	C. pressing
4. cheat	4. harsh	4. pressure	2. A. dreadfully
5. would rather	5. dread	5. regrets	B. dreads
6. pressure	dreaded	6. cheats	C. dreadful
7. cheat	6. harsh	7. dreads	3. A. harshly
8. whisper	7. glance	8. harsh	B. harshness
	8. regrets		C. harsh

			4. A. regrettable
			B. regretful
			C. regrettably
			D. regrets
			regretted
			E. regretfully

Review Test
(pages 217–220)

X.	XI.				
1. healing	1. whisper	1. misbehave	1. b	9. a	17. b
2. would rather	2. praise	2. misunderstood	2. c	10. c	18. c
3. jealous	3. outstanding	3. misprints	3. a	11. c	19. a
4. flaws	4. cheats	4. mistrust	4. d	12. d	20. b
5. scolded	5. stubborn	5. misfortune	5. c	13. d	21. d
6. harsh	6. disappointed	6. mistreats	6. b	14. d	22. c
7. dreads	7. hid	7. misplaced	7. d	15. a	23. d
8. regret	8. refused	8. misled	8. b	16. c	24. a
	refuses				25. b

Unit Three

Seven
A Joy and a Burden (pages 66–75)

I.	III.	V.	VI.	IX.	X.
1. F	1. burden	1. grabbed	1. developed	1. A. moody	1. selfish
2. T	2. tickled	2. developing	2. burden	B. mood	2. bookish
3. F	3. crawled	3. choking	3. peeked	C. moodiness	3. foolish
4. T	4. mood	4. peeked	4. grabbed	mood	4. Polish
5. F	5. tickling	5. grab	5. choke	2. A. ticklish	5. stylish
6. F	6. burden	6. peek	6. crawled	B. tickle	6. girlish
7. T	7. mood	7. develop	7. mood	3. A. burdensome	7. slavish
8. T	8. crawl	8. choking	8. tickling	B. burden	8. Jewish
9. F				4. A. developer	
10. T				B. developmental	
				C. develop	
				D. development	

Eight
A Job and the Threat of a Strike (pages 76–85)

III.	V.	VI.	IX.	X.
1. expire	1. avert	1. gap	1. A. expiration	1. modernize
2. hike	2. negotiating	2. avert	B. expires	2. legalize
3. seeking	3. faded	3. hike	2. A. rejected	3. A. maximize
4. rejected	4. gap	4. reject	B. rejection	B. minimize
5. hike	5. negotiated	5. expires	3. A. negotiations	4. memorize
6. expired	6. averted	6. seeking	B. negotiable	5. emphasized
7. rejects	7. gaps	7. negotiating	C. negotiate	6. hospitalized
8. seek	8. fading	8. fading	4. A. averse	7. criticize
			B. averted	
			C. aversion	

Nine
A Good Husband with Some Bad Habits (pages 86–96)

I.	III.	V.	VI.	IX.
1. T	1. chores	1. nags	1. mind	1. A. sparing
2. T	chore	2. mind	2. gossip	B. sparingly
3. F	2. leak	3. shade	3. spare	C. spare
4. F	3. spare	4. gossip	4. chores	2. A. leaky
5. F	4. digging	5. mind	5. nag	B. leak
6. F	5. spare	6. shade	6. leak	C. leakage
7. T	6. leaking	7. gossip	7. dig	leak
8. T	7. chore	8. nagging	8. shade	3. A. shady
9. T	8. digging			B. shade
10. F				C. shadiness
				shade

X.	XI.	Review Test (pages 221–224)		
1. seeking	1. mind	1. marriage	1. b	9. a	17. b
2. gap	2. fading	2. mileage	2. a	10. c	18. c
3. peeked	3. hike	3. bandage	3. d	11. c	19. c
4. chore	4. shade	4. orphanage	4. b	12. b	20. d
5. avert	5. choked	5. postage	5. c	13. d	21. a
6. negotiate	6. rejected	6. voltage	6. d	14. a	22. b
7. developing	7. expires	7. storage	7. c	15. b	23. c
8. gossip	8. spared	8. percentage	8. b	16. b	24. d
					25. b

Unit Four

Ten
A Police Detective (pages 98–107)

III.	V.	VI.	IX.	X.
1. halt	1. sink	1. bet	1. A. halting	1. simplify
2. scar	2. begged	2. weapons	B. halt	2. purify
3. bet	3. witnesses	3. begged	C. haltingly	3. solidify
4. wound	4. weapons	4. halt	2. A. better	4. terrified
5. scar	5. begging	5. sank	bettor	5. beautify
6. halt	6. sank	6. witnesses	B. bet	6. falsified
7. wounded	7. weapons	7. wound	3. A. unsinkable	7. intensifying
8. bet	8. witnesses	8. scar	B. sank	8. certify
			C. sinkable	
			4. A. beg	
			B. beggar	

Eleven
Becoming a Lawyer (pages 108–118)

I.	III.	V.	VI.	IX.
1. F	1. foes	1. thrill	1. convince	1. A. shrewdly
2. T	2. convinced	2. selfish	2. frowned	B. shrewdness
3. F	3. shrewd	3. boast	3. diminish	C. shrewd
4. F	4. frowned	4. diminishing	4. thrilled	2. A. convincingly
5. T	5. shrewd	5. selfish	5. foe(s)	B. convinced
6. T	6. foes	6. diminished	6. selfish	C. convincing
7. F	7. frown	7. thrilled	7. boast	3. A. selfishly
8. T	8. convince	8. boast	8. shrewd	B. unselfishness
9. F				C. selfish
10. T				D. unselfishly
				E. selfishness
				F. unselfish

X.

1. scholarship
2. leadership
3. partnership
4. citizenship
5. companionship
6. championship
7. relationship
8. membership

IX. (continued)

4. A. boastfully
   B. boastful
   C. boast
   D. boaster
5. A. thrill
   B. thriller

Twelve
A Stockbroker (pages 119–129)

III.	V.	VI.	IX.	
1. plunging	1. peaks	1. invested	1. A. investments	4. A. peak
2. grim	2. bounced	2. peak	B. investing	B. peaked
3. investing	3. pattern	3. swift	C. investor	5. A. bouncer
4. soared	4. swift	4. soared	2. A. grimly	B. bounced
5. grim	5. bounce	5. pattern	B. grimness	6. A. swiftly
6. soaring	6. peak	6. bounce	C. grim	B. swift
7. invests	7. swift	7. grim	3. A. plunger	C. swiftness
8. plunged	8. pattern	8. plunged	B. plunged	

X.		XI.		Review Test (pages 225–228)		
1. wounds	1. foes	1. fatherhood	1. d	9. c	17. a
2. convince	2. grim	2. neighborhood	2. b	10. a	18. c
3. bets	3. halted	3. statehood	3. c	11. b	19. d
4. shrewd	4. sink	4. childhood	4. c	12. d	20. c
5. thrill	5. swift	5. manhood	5. a	13. c	21. b
6. peak	6. selfish	6. priesthood	6. b	14. b	22. a
7. pattern	7. soared	7. motherhood	7. d	15. b	23. d
8. plunging	8. diminishing	8. bachelorhood	8. b	16. d	24. c
					25. d

Unit Five

Thirteen
The Commonwealth of Puerto Rico (pages 132–141)

I.	III.	V.	VI.	IX.	X.
1. F	1. fond of	1. drought	1. flood	1. A. scarcely	1. colonialism
2. T	2. coping	2. drown	2. flee	B. scarce	2. tourism
3. F	3. sweat	3. fled	3. drowned	C. scarcity	3. patriotism
4. F	4. scarce	4. flood	4. drought	2. A. sweater	4. favoritism
5. T	5. cope	5. fleeing	5. scarce	B. sweaty	5. journalism
6. T	6. fond of	6. drought	6. cope	C. sweat	6. Catholicism
7. F	7. scarce	7. flooded	7. fond	3. A. fondly	7. Communism
8. F	8. sweats	8. drowns	8. sweat	B. fondled	8. terrorism
9. T				C. fondness	
10. T				D. fond	

Fourteen
From Ponce to New York (pages 142–154)

III.	V.	VI.	IX.	X.
1. sighed	1. tools	1. stern	1. A. merger	1. A. break
2. pump	2. lack	2. lack	B. merge	B. brake
3. split	3. stern	3. tools	2. A. split	2. A. I
4. merges	4. shiver	4. merge	B. splitting	B. eye
5. pump	5. lacks	5. split	3. A. sternly	3. A. wood
6. split	6. tools	6. shivering	B. stern	B. would
7. merge	7. shivering	7. sighed	C. sternness	4. A. weak
8. sighed	8. stern	8. pump	1. A. meet	B. week
			B. meat	5. A. hear
			2. A. to	B. here
			B. too	6. A. weigh
			C. two	B. way
			3. A. their	7. A. hole
			B. there	B. whole
			4. A. for	8. A. who's
			B. four	B. whose
			5. A. no	9. A. close
			B. know	B. clothes
			6. A. one	10. A. new
			B. won	B. knew
			7. A. ate	
			B. eight	
			8. A. be	
			B. bee	
			9. A. dear	
			B. deer	
			10. A. right	
			B. write	

Fifteen
At Home in Two Lands (pages 155–168)

I.

1. T
2. T
3. F
4. F
5. T
6. F
7. F
8. T
9. F
10. T

III.

1. feud
2. ordeal
3. sort
4. according to
5. sort
6. feud
7. ordeal
8. according to

V.

1. concealed
2. assets
3. melt
4. range
5. melted
6. concealed
7. range
8. asset

VI.

1. ranging
2. conceal
3. according to
4. feud
5. melted
6. asset
7. ordeal
8. sorts

IX.

1. A. accord
   B. in accordance
   C. according to
   D. accordingly
2. A. molten
   B. melted
   melts
3. A. rangy
   B. range
   C. rangers
4. A. conceal
   B. concealment

X.

1. range
2. sort
3. feuding
4. flee
5. merge
6. shivering
7. flood
8. cope

1. fond of
2. scarce
3. drought
4. lacks
5. melts
6. conceal
7. stern
8. split

XI.

1. A. mail
   B. male
2. A. peak
   B. peek
3. A. heal
   B. heel
4. A. bare
   B. bear
5. A. flower
   B. flour
6. A. soar
   B. sore
7. A. plane
   B. plain
8. A. where
   B. wear
9. A. so
   B. sew
10. A. do
    B. due
    C. dew

1. A. hire
   B. higher
2. A. flee
   B. flea
3. A. flu
   B. flew
4. A. pair
   B. pear
5. A. stare
   B. stair
6. A. sale
   B. sail
7. A. piece
   B. peace
8. A. which
   B. witch
9. A. steel
   B. steal
10. A. waste
    B. waist

Review Test
(pages 229–232)

1. c
2. b
3. d
4. c
5. d
6. a
7. b
8. d
9. c
10. d
11. b
12. a
13. c
14. b
15. c
16. d
17. a
18. d
19. c
20. b
21. a
22. c
23. d
24. b
25. c

Unit Six

Sixteen
A Widow and a Dream (pages 170–181)

III.
1. curtail
2. pleaded
3. astonished
4. link
5. pleaded
6. linked
7. astonished
8. curtailed

V.
1. shattered
2. shortage
3. idle
4. on the verge of
5. shortage
6. shattered
7. on the verge of
8. idle

VI.
1. shortage
2. on the verge of
3. link
4. curtail
5. shattered
6. plead
7. astonished
8. idle

IX.
1. A. linked
   B. linkage
2. A. astonishment
   B. astonishingly
   C. astonished
   D. astonishing
3. A. plea(s)
      pleading
   B. pleaded
   C. pleading
      pleas
4. A. shatterproof
   B. shattered
5. A. shorten
   B. shortage
   C. shortly
   D. short
6. A. idly
   B. idleness
   C. idle

X.
1. ringing
2. fan
3. fine
4. mines
5. kind
6. can
7. pitcher
8. box
9. fan
10. pitchers
11. fine
12. box
13. mine
14. kinds
15. can
16. ring

Seventeen
Dan's Irish Rose (pages 182–193)

I.
1. T
2. F
3. F
4. T
5. F
6. T
7. T
8. F
9. T
10. F

III.
1. clinging
2. wandered
3. nodded
4. feeble
5. wander
6. feeble
7. nod
8. clings

V.
1. steer
2. resented
   resent
3. elderly
4. steep
5. resent
6. elderly
7. steers
8. steep

VI.
1. elderly
2. feeble
3. clings
4. resents
5. nods
6. steep
7. wandering
8. steer

IX.
1. A. feebleness
   B. feebly
   C. feeble-minded
   D. feeble
2. A. wanderer
   B. wanderlust
   C. wandered
3. A. eldest
   B. elderliness
   C. elderly
   D. elders
4. A. steeply
   B. steepness
   C. steep
5. A. resentfully
   B. resentment
   C. resentful
   D. resent
      resented

X.
1. last
2. likes
3. well
4. stories
5. seconds
6. will
7. still
8. tip
9. well
10. story
11. last
12. still
13. second
14. tip
15. will
16. like

Eighteen
A Marriage Proposal (pages 194–206)

III.

1. linger
2. greedy
3. strolled
4. flattering
5. greedy
6. lingering
7. flattered
8. stroll

V.

1. leaping
2. bold
3. stunned
4. lull
5. bold
6. leap
7. lull
8. stunned

VI.

1. lull
2. linger
3. greedy
4. stroll
5. bold
6. stunned
7. flattered
8. leap

IX.

1. A. greed
   B. greedy
   C. greedily
2. A. flattering
   B. flattery
   C. flatterer
   D. flatters
      flattered
3. A. stroller
   B. stroll
4. A. lullaby
   B. lull
5. A. stunning
   B. stunned
   C. stunningly
6. A. boldness
   B. boldly
   C. bold

X.

1. stroll
2. curtail
3. steered
4. leapt
   leaped
5. shattered
6. flattering
7. link
8. stunned

1. shortage
2. idle
3. resent
4. greedy
5. elderly
6. feeble
7. linger
8. bold

XI.

1. pro
2. ads
3. lab
4. subs
5. bike
6. mod
7. limo
8. med school
9. hippos
10. champ
11. memo
12. prof
13. condo
14. ref
15. fridge
16. vet
17. phys ed
18. typos
19. reps
20. sub

Review Test
(pages 233–236)

1. b	9. a	17. b
2. a	10. c	18. c
3. c	11. b	19. c
4. d	12. c	20. d
5. b	13. b	21. d
6. c	14. d	22. b
7. d	15. c	23. d
8. d	16. a	24. a
		25. c